PACK UP
YOUR
TROUBLES

PACK UP YOUR TROUBLES

CANADIAN WAR HUMOUR

COMPILED BY
ERIC MANSIKKA

CARTOONS BY PAUL GOMIRATTO

METHUEN
Toronto New York London Sydney Auckland

Dedicated to my parents Vilho and Sivia, my brother Eino, and my children Patrick and Maritta.

Canadian Cataloguing in Publication Data

Main entry under title:

Pack up your troubles : Canadian war humour

ISBN 0-458-81230-7

1. World War, 1939-1945 – Canada. 2. World War, 1939-1945 – Humor. 3. Canadian wit and humor. I. Mansikka, Eric.

D745.2.P32 1987 940.54'0971'0207 C87-094256-5

Printed and bound in Canada

1 2 3 4 87 91 90 89 88

PREFACE

Humour has always risen from the most painful human experiences. It is not surprising that in the stress and turbulence of World War II, human nature prevailed and printing presses routinely published anecdotes and jokes based on the experiences of military life. Humour in a wartime atmosphere is as vital as the daily news: it softens the dehumanizing aspects of war and releases the tensions of day-to-day uncertainty, encouraging the reader to make the best of an unpleasant situation. Naturally humour was directed toward the enemy, but often it was also turned toward living conditions and the military structure itself. While many amenities, and even necessities, were rationed, humour was in full supply to compensate for the constant misery.

Canadians' heroism and sacrifice in World War II have been documented in many excellent books. I chose to look for a lighter aspect of wartime life. I saw humour as a ray of light shining through the black cloud that hung over the fronts at home and on the battlefield.

The material for this collection came from a variety of sources: news wires, bulletins and daily, weekly and bi-monthly publications. Weekly newspapers such as *Khaki*, *The Maple Leaf* and *Wings Abroad* were printed in several countries, i.e. Canada, Italy and Great Britain. Daily news bulletins such as *The "Big 2" Bugle* and *The Column Courier* often were printed right on the front lines.

In preparing this book it was my intention that the reader look back and remember the good times along with the bad. And those of us who did not experience the war will realize the richness of Canadian humour in difficult circumstances.

Eric Mansikka
Sudbury, Ontario

ACKNOWLEDGEMENTS

I wish to thank the following institutions and their staffs for their cooperation and help during the research for this book:

Library, Canadian War Museum
Public Archives of Canada
Directorate of History, National Defence Headquarters
National Library of Canada
Inco Ltd., Public Relations Department
The Canadian Red Cross Society
Sudbury Public Library
Toronto Public Library
Ontario Provincial Command, Royal Canadian Legion

I also wish to thank the following people for their help in preparing the book: Marilyn Harper, Chuck Mossey, Maritta Mansikka and Patrick Mansikka.

Special thanks to Mirja Sariola, Lynn McIvor and Maija-Liisa Mansikka for their help with typing, sketches and proofreading, and to Paul Gomiratto, who drew the cartoons.

E.M.

SHELL LABELS

Jerry was sending a lot of dirt over the other day, a good percentage of which was kerwhomping in the vicinity of a bridge the engineers were building.

"Shells," said one of the engineers. "They don't bother me. Ya don't hafta worry unless one of 'em has your name on it."

"It's not the babies labelled with my monicker I'm worrying about," confided his pal. "It's them babies that're labelled 'To Whom It May Concern.'"

The Maple Leaf, Italy Edition, 1944

Homer says those 25-pounder shells he sees piled up all over the countryside look like accidents on their way to happen!

The Maple Leaf, Italy Edition, 1944

All around the mulberry bush steered the thoughtless tanker.
Saw no need for checking her speed—
Pop! Someone sank her.

RCNMR, 1942

NOTES TO NEWCOMERS
—Stirrup pumps are not for inflating tires.
—Thinners aren't for washing down aircraft.
—Because there are two mag switches it doesn't means there are two engines.
—Ice picks aren't for cleaning radiators.
—Gun-firing buttons not to be tested on daily inspections.

Wings Abroad, 1941

One of the boys explained his plight in a note written home, in exactly four words: "Long time no she."

The "Big 2" Bugle, 1944

Give an example of a collective noun—Garbage-can.

The Beaver Quill, 1942

Gee, I was out with a swell sailor last night. Think he must be a Chief Petting Officer.

CWAC News Letter, 1945

VICKERS .303 MACHINE GUN MARK I
The Vickers was classed as a medium weapon, and could be fired at high or low angles using a tripod. It operated on a gas-assisted recoil system and was water cooled. The Vickers used .303 ammunition fed by belts. Its accurate range was 1100 yards. Canadians used the Vickers .303 in both world wars.

Captain: "A report can be written in such a manner that even the most ignorant can understand it."
Pretty Sergeant: "Yes, Sir. What part is it you don't understand?"

CWAC News letter, 1945

Gunner: "The enemy are thick as peas. What shall we do?"
Lieutenant: "Shell them, you fool, shell them."

CWAC News letter, 1945

Private Penelope says that she is going to try to give up Church parades during Lent.

CWAC News Letter, 1945

She: "Do you always take the other girls for such a long ride?"
Corporal Chapman: "No, it isn't always necessary."

The "Big 2" Bugle, 1944

Corporal Dubord: "I hear you got rid of your old car, sir."
Flight Lieutenant Little: "Yes. it was hopeless. Every time I parked it along would come a cop and ask me if I had reported the accident."

Wings Abroad, 1941

An old maid is a gal who is hungry for love and doesn't know where her next meal is coming from.

The "Big 2" Bugle, 1944

We have just discovered a pilot who forgets his chute, takes off across the flare path, and lands without navigation lights. He must have started life as a plumber.

Wings Abroad, 1941

MO: "After this, keep your hands off my girl, see?"
Masseur: "But I can't resist the desire to give her my massage of love."

The "Big 2" Bugle, 1944

CSM Hess: "Do you know the secret of popularity?"
ATS: "Yes, but mother said I mustn't."

The "Big 2" Bugle, 1944

She was only a taxi driver's daughter, but you auto meter.

The "Big 2" Bugle, 1944

Homer pointed to a vehicle owned by a well-known Canadian general. "That," he said, "is a Vokes-vagen!"

The Maple Leaf, Italy Edition, 1944

Private: "I can't see what keeps you girls from freezing."
Girl: "You're not supposed to."

VICKERS SUPERMARINE SPITFIRE
The Spitfire was a descendant of the S-B6, the 400 mph prewar racing plane designed by Reginald Mitchell. The Spitfire was produced in 22 marks, undergoing some 40 major changes raising its power 100%, rate of climb 80% and top speed from 355 to 454 mph. It was of all-metal stressed-skin construction. Armanent varied.

Try showing your appreciation of your wife, even if it does frighten her at first.

The Tank, 1943

Sergeant-Major Gould: "How long have you been working in Admin Orderly Room?"
New Private Clerk: "Ever since I saw you coming down the hall way."

The Beret, 1946

Axis prisoners in Canada have elected, as their favourite song, "I Don't Get Around Much Anymore."

Khaki, 1943-1944

A small boy was leading a donkey past an army camp. Some soldiers standing nearby decided to have fun with the lad. One of them said: "Say, sonny, why are you holding your brother so tight?" The kid just grinned. "So he won't join the army, soldier," he replied. "That's all."

Khaki, 1943-1944

AND THEN THERE'S THE LITTLE MORON WHO:
—Ate a detonator so that his hair would grow in bangs.
—Took his nose apart to see what made it run.
—Was modest and went into the clothes closet to change his mind.
—Went to a burlesque to see a comic strip.
—Fell through a screen-door and strained himself.
—Described a transparent woman as a cellophane bag.
—Cut off his hands so he could play the piano by ear.
—Covered his pay envelope with iodine because he'd heard his pay was to be cut.
—Ran around the corn flakes box because it said: "Tear around here."

Khaki, 1943-1944

DIFFERENT
Overheard in an air raid shelter during a black-out:
He: Somehow your kisses seem different tonight, Mary.
She: Maybe it's just because my name is Violet.

The Tank, 1943

"Now, Trickey," said Flight Sergeant Brown, "can you tell me what a hypocrite is?"

"Yes, Flight," replied Trickey. "It's an airman who comes on early morning readiness with a smile on his face."

Wings Abroad, 1941

For the readers of "The Tank," war today is a matter of "mud, sweat and gears."

The Tank, 1941

Mr. Tom Poolereigh, of the Ministry for the Coordination of Suspense, tells me that by regularly shaving the hairs of the lower legs whiskers may be produced, on which the socks may be hooked.

The Tank, 1941

Jack and Jill showed sense until
They opened wide the scuttle
Showed a light—Fritz pipped them right
and Jack had no rebuttal.

RCNMR, 1942

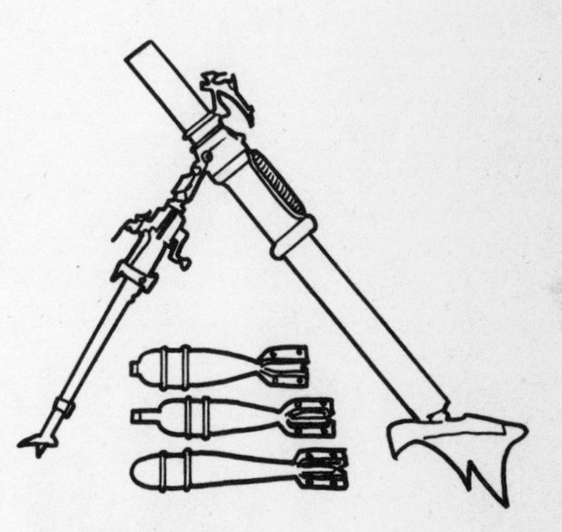

3-INCH MORTAR
The 3-inch was the standard heavy infantry motar. It could hit targets as close as 125 yards, or a maximum of 2800 yards. A crew of three transported it in a Universal Carrier and man-handled it in three parts. Eventually the army used three types: the 4.2-inch, the 3-inch and the 2-inch mortar.

THE MORTAR BOMB
The mortar could fire three types of bombs: smoke, high explosive and star. The 4.2-inch fired a 20-pound bomb, the 3-inch a 10-pound and the 2-inch a $2^1/_2$ -pound bomb.

..."and when those shells came over I just pulled my pants up and ran for cover. They should dig those things under shelter."

Front-Line Charlie says: "I was up to brigade today: right up."
The Maple Leaf, Italy Edition, 1944

CWAC: My husband's in the navy, so be careful.
GI Wolf: "Ah, ha! So your anchor's aweigh!"
CWAC News Letter, 1944

After the war I'll NEVER
Wake with the dawn,
Carry my cutlery in my handbag all day,
Say "Yes, Ma'm" or "No, Sir."
CWAC News Letter, 1944

"Hey, Toots, a skunk's got two stripes, hasn't it?"
"No, dear. You're thinking of the corporal."
CWAC News Letter, 1944

CWAC: "I wrote a True Confession story once."
WREN: "Was it bought?"
CWAC: "No, but the editor came all the way from New York to meet me."
CWAC News Letter, 1944

JUST A RUMOUR
"As soon as we get on the boat to go over, we will get rum every day like the sailors."
The Tank, 1941

PICCADILLY
In a town occupied by Canadians they have given Canadian names to piazzas and casas. The tallest building has been labelled "Sun Life Building" and the big piazza "Dominion Square." Just then what must be the most beautiful blonde signorina in all Italy ankled by.

Said a soldier to his pal, "Looks more like Piccadilly Circus."
The Maple Leaf, Italy Edition, 1944

EXTRACT BY THE EXPERTS.
NO. 1: KNOW YOUR DRILL!
"Trewp! Trewpshan! Trewpwllturnlift… leeeft… tan! By thsentah… Queeeack… match!… Liftroitliftroitlift! Trewpwlltaaaarnabeeeyout… aaaabeeyout… tann! Chickwantoofreefourwadd, Chestahtchininarmfrunterear! Trewp… alt!"
The Tank, 1941

Mussolini kicks at Britain's Blockade—since soap has become a scarcity he can't get Greece off his hands.
Wings Abroad, 1941

In the sergeants Mess: "Do you serve crabs here?"
"We serve anyone – sit down."

The orderly room had received application to wed from four of their strength but two of the names had been misplaced. The very new Orderly Sergeant was given instruction to get the missing names while she was taking morning parade. Filled with abounding zeal the sergeant called the parade to order and then loudly demanded, "Will those girls who want to get married please step forward and give their names". The response was unanimous!

CWAC News Letter, 1944

Little fly upon the wall
Ain't you got no mom or pop at all?
Squish!

Wings Abroad, 1941

She telephoned in great fear:
There's a rat in my room!"
"Send him down," said the desk-clerk.
"He must register."

Khaki, 1944-1945

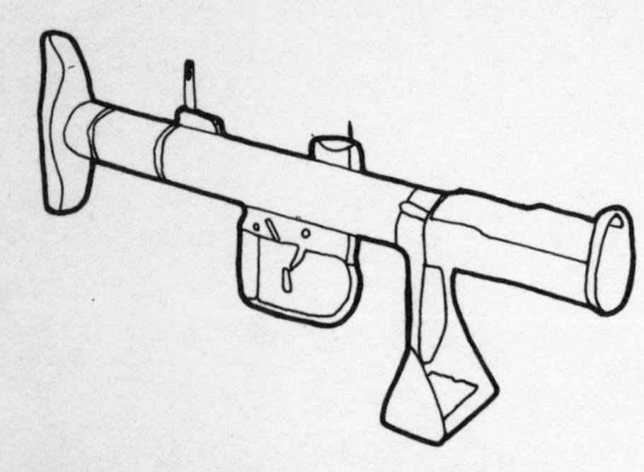

PIAT—PROJECTOR INFANTRY ANTI-TANK
PIAT came into service in 1942. It was shoulder fired and was a kind of cross between a bazooka and an anti-tank rifle. The launcher weighed approximately 32 pounds

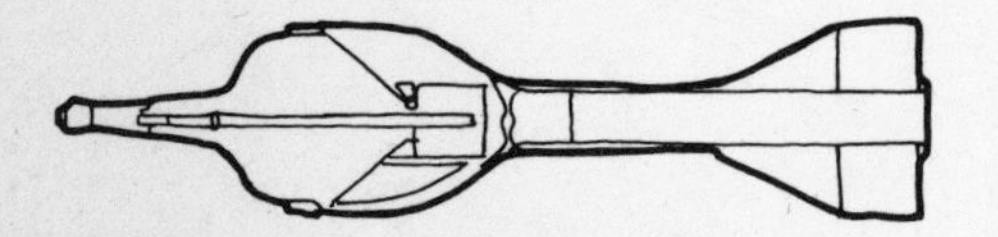

The bomb or rocket weighed 2½ pounds and contained a charge of high explosives. It was effective to within 100 yards against armour, vehicles and pillboxes.

OFF THE RECORD
Taylor… "Hasn't that girl got a lovely face, Jimmy?"
McCullough: "Don't rush me, Ernie, I haven't reached that far yet."

The "Big 2" Bugle, 1944

Said he: "Darling, when I look into your face time stands still."
He's still wondering why she refuses to speak to him.

The "Big 2" Bugle, 1944

Pa: "It's two o'clock. About time Sergeant Lohnes went home and Sally came to bed."
Ma: "Now then, Pa, just remember how we used to court."
Pa: "That settles it; out he goes!"

Khaki, 1944–45

A Scotchman was told that his wife needed salt air—so he fanned her with a herring!

Khaki, 1944–1945

What happens to Hitler when he takes off his boots?
He smells defeat!

Khaki, 1944–1945

Ding Dong Bell,
Someone's blown to hell.
Who blew him up?
Maybe Bertha Krupp.
What a naughty boy was he
To overlook he had D.G.

RCNMR, 1942

We don't mind the promulgation of new ideas on how to win the war in any situation, no matter how much it interferes with us personally—but when the cooks attempt the creation of a new double-resistance armour plating, and try it out on us in the form of pie pastry, we draw the line.

Wings Abroad, 1941

First She: "Does your husband talk in his sleep?"
Second She: "No, and it's terribly exasperating. He just grins."

The "Big 2" Bugle, 1944

Corporal Hayward (hearing crash from Priory kitchen): "More dishes, Roy?"
Roy: "No—less."

Wings Abroad, 1941

"Her uniform looks as if she had been poured into it and forgot to say "when".

Flattery is 90 per cent soap. And soap is 90 per cent lye.

Wings Abroad, 1941

An incinerator is a person who hints things about you instead of coming right out and telling you.

The Beaver Quill, 1944

Question—
What did the sweet potato say to the radio announcer?
Answer—
You're just a common 'tater.

Wings Abroad, 1941

Airman: "Listen to him squawk over three smokes."
Corporal: "It's not the three smokes, but the three every ten minutes."

Wings Abroad, 1941

A bachelor is a man who never makes the same mistake once.

The Tank, 1943

This is how U-packs were disposed for their attacks in echelon.

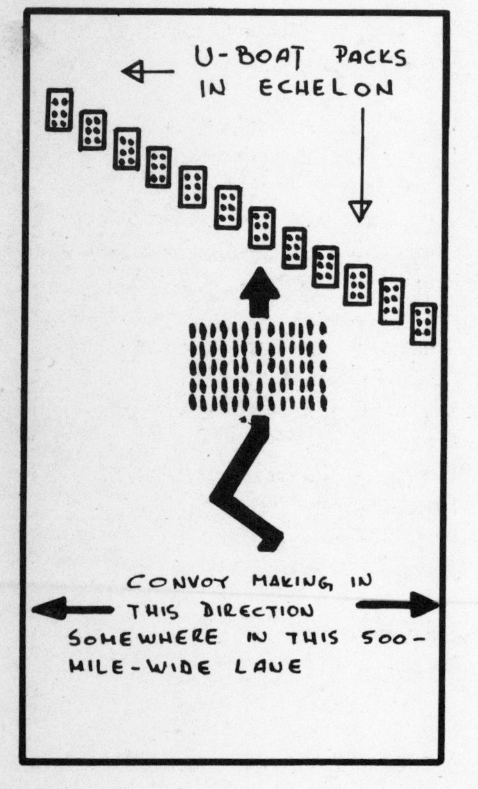

A Japanese spy reported to his superiors in Tokyo as follows: "We will win the war because the people of Canada are starving. Whenever two honourable Canadians meet they clasp hands and say in unison
'WHAT'S COOK'N'."

CWAC News Letter, 1944

A bow-legged CWAC named Keys
Had plenty of room between knees
When she came to attention
Her sergeant did mention
Her knees were still standing at ease.

CWAC News Letter, 1944

CWAC: "Boy, what a stepper! Did you ever take dancing lessons?"
Private: "No, but I've studied wrestling."

CWAC News Letter, 1944

BEST SELLER
Somebody has an idea for the title of new book: "The Road to Rome—Blow by Blow."

"Should be a best seller," commented a sapper, who was putting the finishing touches on a new bridge.

The Maple Leaf, Italy Edition, 1944

THAT WILL BE THE DAY WHEN—
—The boys quit swiping the padre's ink out of the reading room.
—The NAAFI canteen puts meat in the sausage rolls.
—The coal man screens all the dust from our coal issue.
—Someone tells the truth about receiving a black eye.
—The NAAFI canteen goes bankrupt through undercharging the troops.

Wings Abroad, 1941

Sergeant Hamilton (interviewing applicants for concert party): "Have you ever had any stage experience?"
Rookie: "Well, I had my leg in a cast once."

The Tank, 1940

The Education Officer was quizzing the class about history. "What was Louis the XIV chiefly responsible for?" she asked.

The little blonde CWAC had been dreaming away in her corner. "Louis the XV," she said with a far-away look.

CWAC News Letter, 1945

Some folks live and learn, but some folks just live.

CWAC News Letter, 1945

ABBREVIATIONS

A.D.G.B.	Air Defence of Great Britain
A.V.R.E.	Assault vehicle, Royal Engineers
Bde.	Brigade
B.E.F.	British Expeditionary Force
B.S.T.	British summer time
C.A.	Civil Affairs
C.A.O.F.	Canadian Army Occupation Force
Capt.	Captain
C.B.	Companion of the Order of the Bath
C.B.E.	Commander of the Order of the British Empire
Cdn.	Canadian
C.G.S.	Chief of the General Staff
C.-in-C.	Commander-in-Chief
C.M.G.	Companion of the Order of St. Michael and St. George
C.M.H.Q.	Canadian Military Headquarters, London
Col.	Colonel
COSSAC	Chief of Staff, Supreme Allied Commander
C.O.T.C.	Canadian Officers Training Corps
C.S.M.	Company sergeant-major
C.W.A.C.	Canadian Women's Army Corps
D.C.M.	Distinguished Conduct Medal
Div.	Division
D.S.O.	Companion of the Distinguished Service Order
E.D.	Canadian Efficiency Decoration
F.B.M.	Feet board measure
G.C.M.G.	Knight Grand Cross of the Order of St. Michael and St. George
Gen.	General
G.H.Q.	General Headquarters
G.O.C.	General Officer Commanding
G.O.C.-in-C.	General Officer Commanding-in-Chief
G.S.	General Staff
H.E.	High explosive
H.L.I. (of C.)	The Highland Light Infantry of Canada
H.M.C.S.	His Majesty's Canadian Ship
H.M.S.	His Majesty's Ship
Hon.	Honourable
Inf.	Infantry
Lieut. (Lt.)	Lieutenant
L.M.G.	Light machine gun
L. of C.	Lines of communication
Maj.	Major
M.B.E.	Member of the Order of the British Empire
M.C.	Military Cross
M.G.	Machine gun
M.M.	Military Medal
NAAFI	Navy Army Air Forces Institute
N.C.O.	Non-commissioned officer
N.R.M.A.	National Resources Mobilization Act
O.B.E.	Officer of the Order of the British Empire
PIAT	Projector, infantry anti-tank
Pte.	Private
R.A.F.	Royal Air Force
R.A.M.C.	Royal Army Medical Corps
R.C.A.	Royal Canadian Artillery
R.C.A.F.	Royal Canadian Air Force
R.C.A.M.C.	Royal Canadian Army Medical Corps
R.C.E.	Corps of Royal Canadian Engineers
R.C.H.A.	Royal Canadian Horse Artillery
R.C.N.	Royal Canadian Navy
R.C.R.	The Royal Canadian Regiment
R.D.F.	Radio direction finding
Recce	Reconnaissance or reconnoitering
R.F.C.	Royal Flying Corps
R.H.L.I.	The Royal Hamilton Light Infantry
R.M.C.	Royal Military College
R.N.	Royal Navy
S.A.S.	Special Air Service
S.F.	Special Force
SHAEF	Supreme Headquarters, Expeditionary Force
Sitrep	Situation report
S.S. (British)	Special Service (i.e. Commandos)
S.S. (German)	Schutzstaffeln (plural): originally elite guards of the Nazi party; later used as an independent term; fighting forces of S.S. were known as Waffen S.S. (i.e. Combat S.S.)
Tac.	Tactical
U.S.	United States
U.S.A.	United States Army
V.C.	Victoria Cross
V.D.	Colonial Auxiliary Forces Officers Decoration
W.O.II	Warrant Officer, Class II
W.R.C.N.S.	Women's Royal Canadian Naval Service

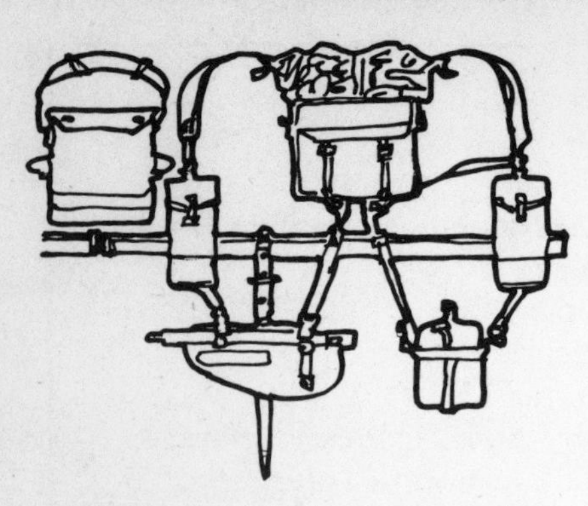

PERSONAL EQUIPMENT—CANADIAN INFANTRYMAN
Canadian uniforms and personal equipment were standardized on the British pattern. Badges of rank were identical to the British. The battle kit included an anti-gas respirator in a haversack, a packsack, ground sheet, full sized spade, water-bottle, pouches for Bren-gun and rifle ammunition and hand grenades.

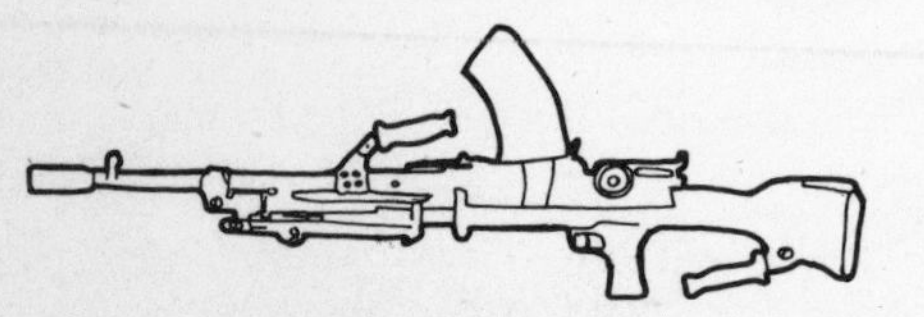

BREN .303 LIGHT MACHINE GUN
The Bren originated in Czechoslovakia as the Brno ZB and was adopted by Britain in 1932. The British improved it, modified it to take .303 rifle ammunition and called it the Bren, a combination of Brno and Enfield, the British arsenal. The Bren could be converted into a heavy machine gun, firing from a tripod mount, or into an anti-aircraft gun. It was also used on vehicles. The Bren weighed 22 pounds, could fire 500 rounds on full automatic and had an effective range of 500 yards. Canada manufactured thousands of these air-cooled, gas-operated weapons.

Sergeant: "I said 'Left turn.' Don't you know left from right?"
Private: "Yes…"
Sergeant: "Yes, what?"
Private: "Yes, Sergeant—but I didn't know right could be wrong."

CWAC News Letter, 1945

"The army is beginning to get me.
Every day I look more and more like the gal on my identification card."

CWAC News Letter, 1945

GLOOMY RUMOUR
"When you get overseas you will be put in quarantine for sixty days." (Well versed "B" Squadron L/Corporal)

The Tank, 1941

BEER PARLOUR DRINKING
Beer should be drunk in three gulps and a two minute silence between orders. This allows the froth to settle through your lapels.

The Beaver Quill, 1942

An old maid school teacher was taking her pupils to the zoo in the spring. Upon arriving at the monkey cages, she inquired why there were no monkeys in sight.

"Well madam," replied the attendant, "in the mating season the pairs retire to the rear of the cage for two or three days.

"But won't they come out for a peanut?"

"Darned if I know ma'am," said the attendant. "Would you?"

The Beaver Quill, 1943

Q1: "At the dance, they tell me, you had powder on your suit."
Q3: "Oh! that's just idle talc."

The Beaver Quill, 1943

SM Brown had a black eye for which the excuse he gave was a car accident.

Yes, apparently hugging the wrong curves.

The Beaver Quill, 1943

Bill: "Would you rather have an ordinary wedding or elope at midnight?"
Phil: "I'll take the ladder."

The Beaver Quill, 1943

Then there was the recruit who thought a "Common-law wife" was one married in quite the ordinary way.

The Beaver Quill, 1943

Indignant MO: "Don't call me doctor! You fellows have been soldiering long enough to know that an officer must be given his title. You know there are no 'doctors' in the army."
Voice from rear rank of sick parade: "You're telling us!"

The Tank, 1940

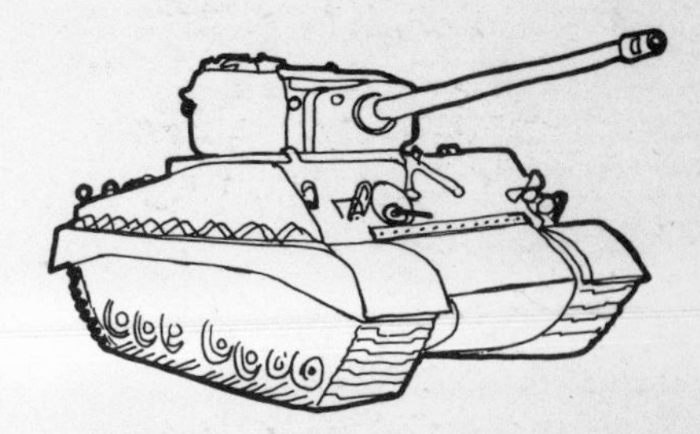

SHERMAN FIREFLY
The Canadian armoured formations used the U.S. M4 medium tank called the General Sherman in Italy and northwest Europe. The early 30-ton Sherman had a crew of five, a speed of 29 mph and a cruising range of 150 miles. It mounted a 75-mm gun and two machine guns. Later Shermans like the Firefly mounted a British 17-pounder or the 105-mm gun.

FIRST INTELLIGENT RUMOUR
"We are not going any place for the winter."

The Tank, 1941

FAMOUS LAST WORDS
"He hasn't any Luftwaffe."

The "Big 2" Bugle, 1944

The mild-mannered little Jill walked casually along. It was her first evening out after three days CB for failing to salute an officer. Suddenly she found herself face to face with the OC, but again her arm failed to rise to the occasion.

"Private Jones," said the OC briskly, "do you still not know that you have to salute an officer?"

"Yes, Ma'm," was the meek reply, "but I didn't want to bother you this time, 'cause I thought you were still mad at me."

CWAC News Letter, 1945

It's hard to find
For love or money
A joke that's clean
And also funny.

CWAC News Letter, 1945

WREN: "I don't think I look thirty, do you, dear?"
CWAC: "No dear, not now. But you used to."

CWAC News Letter, 1945

"What is a lieutenant-commander?"
"A lieutenant's wife.

CWAC News Letter, 1945

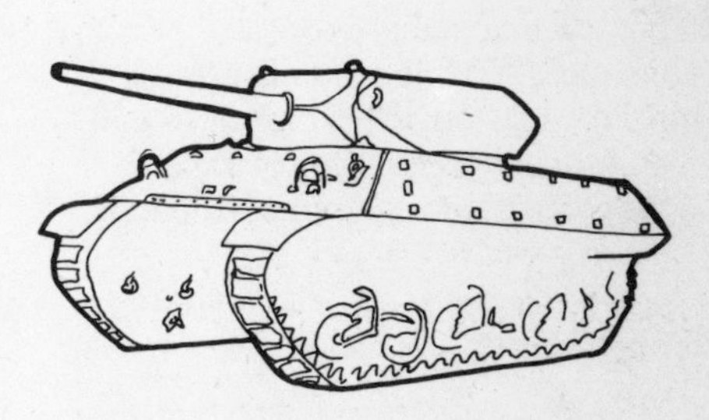

17-POUNDER (SELF-PROPELLED)
The 17-pounder was a British modification of a basic American design. The M1O self-propelled 17-pounder mounted its gun in a Sherman tank chassis with an open turret. It also carried a .50 machine gun for ground or anti-aircraft protection. It was used by anti-tank regiments in support roles.

Corporal: "Are you the CWAC Quartermaster?"
She: "Yes."
Corporal: "Is it true that you supply CWACs?"
She: "That's right."
Corporal: "Good! Supply me with three for tonight."

CWAC News Letter, 1945

BRIGHT RUMOUR
"As soon as we get our tin hats we will also get our trades pay."

The Tank, 1941

OFF THE RECORD
A psychiatrist is a doctor who asks questions to see if infants have more fun in infancy or adults more fun in adultery.

The "Big 2" Bugle, 1944

Dykes to Gair: "What did the earwig say to the airman?"
Gair: "Dunno."
Dykes: "I'm laying all my eggs in your biscuits."

Wings Abroad, 1941

POEM
I shot an arrow into the air,
It fell to earth—I know not where.
I lost ten of the damned things that way!

Wings Abroad, 1941

Cummings: "Would you donate ten cents to the old ladies' home?"
Leppington: "What! They out again?"

Wings Abroad, 1941

VICKERS WELLINGTON
The "Wimpey" was the backbone of Bomber Command before the four-engine heavies took over. It saw service with several Canadian squadrons in all major theatres doing duty in numerous roles, such as mine-laying and clearing, U-boat hunting, photo-reconnaissance and troop transport. The plane was of fabric-covered metal geodetic construction, fabric covered. It had a maximum speed of 235 mph at 15,500 feet. Armament consisted of six .303 guns and a bombload of 4,500 pounds.

Wanted a super man to compete in a gab fest with "Our own Leather."
Which sergeant pilot objects to thorns in connection with roses?
Two pounds for a ride on a motorcycle is a bit steep—ask Patterson, our worthy SP.
Why do the boys all applaud when Buschlen steps into the bus before 8 a.m.?
Flannel Foot O'Brein had better stop praising married life. Stop it, Bob! You'll have us all married if you don't. I'm sure you wouldn't want to have that on your mind.

Wings Abroad, 1941

According to some recent trade test answers, a definition of steam is "Water gone crazy with the heat."

Wings Abroad, 1941

OFF THE RECORD
Mk.1: "You remember when you cured my rheumatism, Doc., a couple of years ago and you told me to avoid dampness?"
MO: "Yes, that's right."
Mk.1: "Well, I've come to ask you if it's alright if I now take a bath."

The "Big 2" Bugle, 1944

Said a very charming young lady recently: "Everything I really want to do is either illegal, immoral or plain fattening."

The Beaver Quill, 1942

Famous Last Words: "Of course I've got the Right-of-Way."

"Get the butt of your rifle into the hollow of your shoulder," cried the instructor.

"I can't," said the recruit. "There's a bone there."

"Oh, is there? I suppose the rest of these blokes are filletted?"

The Beaver Quill, 1942

Said one skeleton to another in a medical museum—
"If we had any guts we'd get out of here."

The Beaver Quill, 1942

Some soldiers who were invited to a party the other day were talking on the telephone to their home folks. "We gotta go to a party tonight," one said. "Really would rather stay in barracks and get some sleep—but we gotta keep up the civilian morale."

The Beaver Quill, 1942

STATISTICAL NOTES
Have you noticed how some fellows can get a commission and still remain normal, while giving some birds ONE STRIPE practically ruins 'em?"

The Beaver Quill, 1942

OPS
The cute young thing entered the doctor's office with a worried look on her face. "Doctor," she said, "I need an operation."

"Major?" asked the doctor.

"No," she said. "Corporal."

Khaki, 1943–1944

CONSOLIDATED CATALINA
During the war some 650 Catalinas were flown by the RCAF and RAF on anti-submarine patrols. The Catalina flying boat entered service with the U.S. Navy in 1936. It was of all-metal stressed-skin construction having an endurance of 14 hours at 100 knots with 2,000-pound bombload.

MURDER
The Messing Officer was sampling the new cook's first soup. He looked up suddenly. "You served in the last war, didn't you?"

"Yes, sir, I served for three years and was wounded twice."

The officer tasted the soup again.

"You're a lucky guy," he said. "It's a wonder they didn't kill you."

Khaki, 1943–1944

LEAVE US LEAVE IT
The girls were talking things over down at the office.

"Gee, Gladys," sez one, "I am tired."

"What's the matter, Mabel?"

"Well, I'll tell you," sez Mabel, "I've been out with a forty-eight hour pass."

Khaki, 1943–1944

THE WINNAH
Private Pashkoodnik staggered back to barracks in an extremely gory condition. As he entered the guard room he was unfortunate enough to walk smack into his CMS.

"Well," growled the WO, "what happened to you?"

"A wise guy in the next company got smart with me, I stuck my nose firmly between his teeth and threw him heavily to the ground."

Khaki, 1943–1944

DOUGLAS DAKOTA
The Douglas Dakota transport plane was a military version of the prewar DC-3 airliner. The plane's main role was to carry troops and supplies wherever needed. It was of all-metal stressed-skin construction. Maximum payload was 9,000 pounds, maximum speed was 230 mph at 8,500 feet and it had a crew of three.

Excerpt from George Dykes' story of his trip from No.1 Fighter to 100 Squadron:—
"…and so we stayed overnight at the village inn, 'The Shakespeare.' Stap me! I really had a good time that night. That's the second time Shakespeare's given me a headache, once in school at home and once in an English village."

Wings Abroad, 1941

A virgin forest is a forest in which the hand of man has never set foot.

The "Big 2" Bugle, 1944

Mazie: "It's funny, you can't keep a boy friend. You're a cute kid."
Lulu: "Yeah, but when I tell 'em Mom's a sergeant they don't seem to like it."

CWAC News Letter, 1944

First corporal: "Well, why didn't you stick up for me in that argument?"
Second corporal: "I did didn't I? He said you weren't fit to lie down with a pig and I told him you were."

Wings Abroad, 1941

THOUGHT FOR THE DAY
Someone once asked the late Bishop Taylor Smith, Chaplain General of the forces, if he knew the right way to heaven.

"Certainly", said the Bishop, "Take the first turn to the right and keep straight on."

The "Big 2" Bugle, 1944

IMAGINATION
A sergeant discovered an intoxicated private leaning heavily against a mess hall.

"What do you think you're doing, soldier?"

"I'm holding up the building." replied the Joe.

"Izzat so?" sneered the sergeant. "Well get going! Scram!"

The private moved way. Sooo—the building collapsed.

Khaki , 1943-44

Service and Auxiliary Personnel could obtain coloured copies of the above and similar posters free for pin-up purposes by applying to "Wings Abroad" RCAF Overseas HQ, London.

OPINIONS

The training plane had gone into a terrific tail-spin. The instructor brought it out with little effort. Then he spoke into the intercom. "I'll bet 50% of the people down there thought we were going to be killed that time."

The student pilot swallowed and replied, "Yes, sir! And 50% of the people up here thought so too!"

Khaki, 1943–1944

The MO said my finger nails
Were longer than they could be.
I said I thought her nose, perhaps,
Was longer than it should be.

CWAC News Letter, 1944

THINGS CERTAIN PEOPLE WOULD LIKE TO KNOW.
What airman says Flight Sergeant Carson is all right in his place, but it hasn't been dug yet?

What Canadian wants to know what will happen if one of these tiny English cars hit a wad of gum?

Wings Abroad, 1941

From Shanghai comes this little tit-bit about a foreign correspondent's report. He wrote:—
This little country is tense tonight as it waits.
This little country is very tense.
This little country is past tense.

Wings Abroad, 1941

Certain evacuees to Canada and the United States complain that our rooms are too warm; oh yeah, they're just not used to having both sides of themselves warm at the same time.

Wings Abroad, 1941

Since the new rations came out,
Never in the history of messing was so little received by so many for so much.

Wings Abroad, 1941

Boughner: "What's that lump in your breast pocket?"
Carter (whispering): "It's dynamite. I'm waiting for Prettie. Every time he sees me he hits me on the chest and breaks my fountain pen. Next time he does it he'll blow his hand off."

Wings Abroad, 1941

1st CWAC, sourly: "I'm nobody's fool."
2nd CWAC, sweetly: "Too bad, darling, maybe some old sugar daddy will adopt you."

CWAC News Letter, 1944

There's holly in my coat lapel,
On my shoe there's mistletoe,
Placed there out of fond regard
For certain folks I know.

CWAC News Letter, 1944

"I'm wearing my old undies and saving my new expensive ones!"

"What for? A rainy day?"

"No, dearie, a windy day."

The Beaten Zone, 1945

TRUCK, 15 CWT., 4 x 4 CHEVROLET
This vehicle was mainly used for wireless communication with Brigade and Divisional Headquarters by the MG Coys, RCE, RCA, and RCEME workshops and other units. The body was all steel, welded, with hinged tailgate and special tarpaulin with brackets for aerial bases. Maximum speed was 47 mph and the average fuel consumption was 13 mpg. It had a 6-cylinder in-line engine.

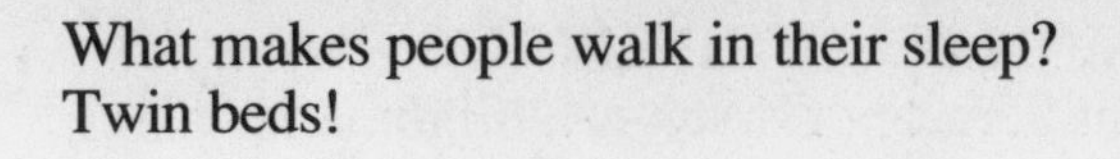

What makes people walk in their sleep?
Twin beds!

The Beaten Zone, 1945

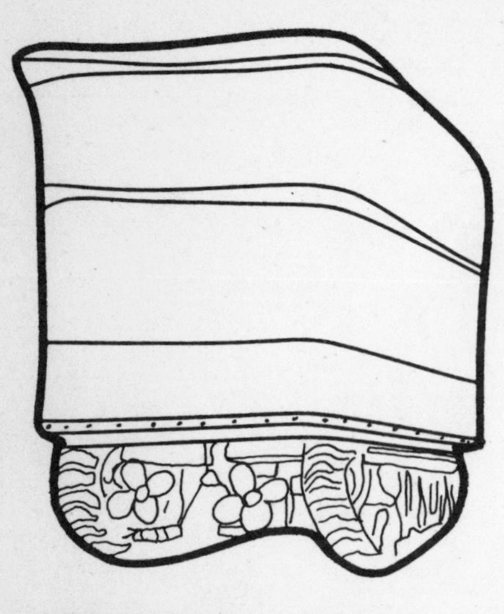

DUPLEX DRIVE (DD) TANK
The troops nicknamed the swimming tanks Donald Duck. They were amphibious Shermans that could make 5 knots in the water. The chassis of the Shermans were waterproofed, fitted with collapsible canvas screen and rubber air tubes. On inflation with compressed air the tubes gave the tank positive buoyancy. The DD was moved by two propellers at the rear. The squadrons of DD tanks were launched by 1st Hussars on D-Day.

She flirted with the butcher playing for bigger steaks.

The Beaten Zone, 1945

Many a man has made a monkey of himself by reaching for the wrong limb.

The Beaten Zone, 1945

Dame May Whitty says: "I've got everything Betty Grable has—only I've had it a little longer."

The Beaten Zone, 1945

TRENCH TALK
Front-Line Charlie says: "Jeez, was I up there today! Where I was ya could hear the echoes of our medium guns. No foolin!"

The Maple Leaf, Italy Edition, 1944

OFF THE RECORD
If Little Red Riding Hood lived today
The modern girl would scorn her
She only had to meet one wolf
Not one in every corner!

The "Big 2" Bugle, 1944

George Dykes—"You're a better man than I am, Gordon's Gin."

Wings Abroad, 1941

SHORTAGES
In recent months the demand for secretaries in NDHQ has become so great that applicants are given only one test. They are put in a room with a sewing machine, a washing machine, an ice cream freezer and a typewriter. If they can pick out the typewriter—they're hired.

Khaki, 1944–1945

HO-HUM
The Joe was very tired. He had just come off a twenty-mile route march. He went into a barber shop and slouched down on the chair.

The barber told him he was sitting too low in the chair for a shave.

"OK," said the soldier wearily, "give me a haircut".

Khaki, 1944–1945

HOPEFUL
Private Pashkoodnik is in the dog house again. The other day he approached his sergeant and enquired:

"Sarge, would you blame me for something I didn't do?"

"Of course not", replied the Sergeant.

"That's very nice", murmured Pashkoodnik, "Y'see, I didn't get up for reveille."

Khaki, 1944–1945

NIGHT CLUB PROBLEM
Two Joes went into a night club, sat down and gazed about them expansively.

"Y'know", said one of the soldiers conversationally,"I like this place. Some night spots take you to Havana, others take you to Brazil and still others to Algiers. This dump just takes you!"

Khaki, 1944–1945

Toscanini: "I kissed my first woman and smoked my first cigarette on the same day. I have never had time for tobacco since."

The Column Courier, 1944–1945

TRENCH TALK
"That Kraut shell came over so close I could smell its breath!"

The Maple Leaf, Italy Edition, 1944

CAUTIOUS, AIN'T HE?
The RSM of a training centre in MD 3 recently received a printed invitation requesting his attendance at the opening of a new sergeants' mess at a nearby camp. He was exceedingly busy, but decided nevertheless to go. Noting the RSVP in the corner of the card, the RSM instructed the assistant of his office to accept for him. The assistant read the invitation very carefully, then replied in all seriousness, "I wouldn't go, Sir, if I were you. That RSVP stands for "Reply and Send Valuable Present."

Khaki, 1944–1945

REMINDER
A voice in the night: "And furthermore, Corporal, this is not one of the four freedoms!"

Khaki, 1944–1945

5.5-INCH GUN/HOWITZER
The 5.5 was used by the Canadians as a medium artillery weapon. It fired an 82-pound high-explosive projectile up to 18,200 yards at a rate of two rounds per minute. It was handled by a 10-man crew and was transported by a 5-ton tractor known as Matador.

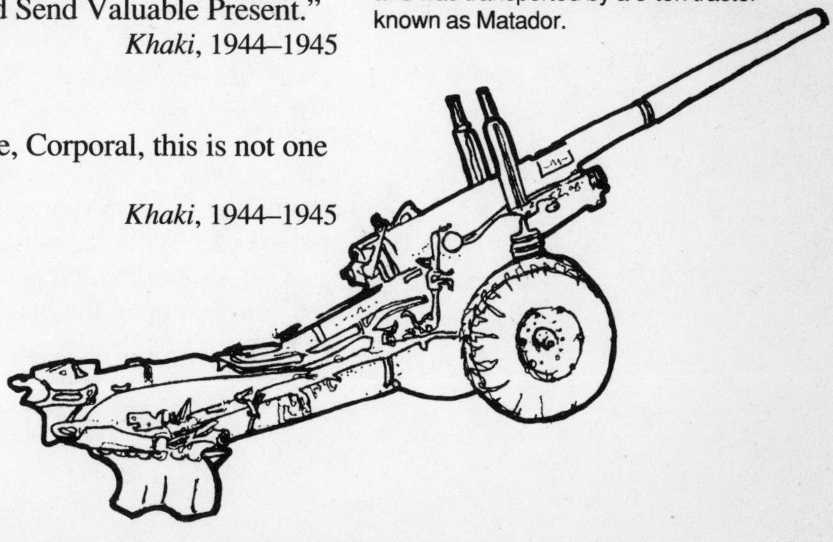

CAR, HEAVY UTILITY, FORD
There were two classes of heavy utilities: civilian type station wagons and military pattern models. The vehicles were issued in limited numbers to army HQs for transporting personnel over suitable terrain. The V-8 engine was rated at 95 hp with a maximum speed of 70 mph and an average fuel consumption of 13 mpg. Canadian and British armies used these vehicles in the Western Desert and Italy. One local modification was the removal of the roof, converting the vehicle to a soft top tourer type having a crew of five including the driver. Fittings included rifle clips, petrol and water cans, tools, map container, first aid kit and ignition with radio interference suppression.

The Education Officer in our district received a telephone call the other day.

"Say, Sir, do grown moths eat wool?"

The EO frowned. "No," he said. "The larvae eat wool—grown moths don't."

Then the voice shouted: "See, moth! What did I tell you! Now spit up my pants!"

Khaki, 1944–1945

RUSH

During the P.T. period a soldier tripped and fell while running around the field. A moment later an instructor came running up and asked: "What happened to you?"

"I've broken my leg and I can't get up", replied the Joe.

"Well," yapped the instructor,"what are you waiting for? Start doing push ups."

Khaki, 1944–1945

She's awful smart; is Private Smith;
They tell her things—she heeds 'em.
She ain't got brains for thinkin with;
In the army she don't need 'em.
Cause she don't have to reason why,
An' wastin' time's a pity;
They tell her when to do or die—
She's awful smart, is Smitty.

CWAC News Letter,1944

TRENCH TALK
"Praise the Lord and pass the lice powder."

The Maple Leaf, Italy Edition, 1944

First CWAC: "I don't want to get married. Men make me sick!"
Second CWAC: "Well, I wouldn't mind getting married but I don't like washing dishes and all that kind of stuff."
Third CWAC: "Gee, I'd love to get married! I'd wash anything!"

CWAC News Letter, 1944

CAR, HEAVY UTILITY, 4 x 2 FORD
The 4 x 2 model shown was an early production type having a British-built body on the basic 8-cwt CMP chassis. The vehicle was used in the personnel carrying role. The rear seats could be folded down to provide extra cargo space. It carried a crew of six, including the driver, and had a 95 hp V-8 engine.

Front-Line Charlie says: "I'm getting tired of this rear area stuff. I want a transfer to a real combat outfit. Think I'll try to team up with the Anti Malarial Combat Unit."

The Maple Leaf, Italy Edition, 1944

ENGLISH VINTAGE
Boss: "I'm surprised at you. Do you know what they do with boys who tell lies?"
Office Boy: "Yes, sir; when they get old enough the firm sends them out as salesmen."

The Column Courier, 1944–1945

Did you hear about the little moron with literary ambitions who committed suicide so that he could become a ghost writer.

CWAC News Letter, 1944

Captain Smith: "I have six children. First comes Millie, my daughter."
Lieutenant Jones: "And who comes after Millie?"
Captain Smith: "The whole Canadian army."

CWAC News Letter, 1944

Front-Line Charlie says: "I'll never see one of those actions again, the Canadian army newsreels of Ortona were simply terrifying."

The Maple Leaf, Italy Edition, 1944

A kiss that speaks volumes is seldom a first edition.

The "Big 2" Bugle, 1944

INSURANCE
The soldier wrote to his young bride: "Darling, come down next Sunday if you possibly can. Also, I am short of cash, so please bring me $10.00". Then. "PS—If you can't come, send me $12.00."

Khaki, 1944–1945

"MOTHER"
Mother 'tis your face I see,
Whenever grief envelops me.
If only I could linger near
To kiss your lips, to dry your tear.

It will be you and you alone
Who captures me when I come home.
Then 'twill be a face of smiles,
For I'll be home for quite awhile.

R.S.
Khaki, 1944–1945

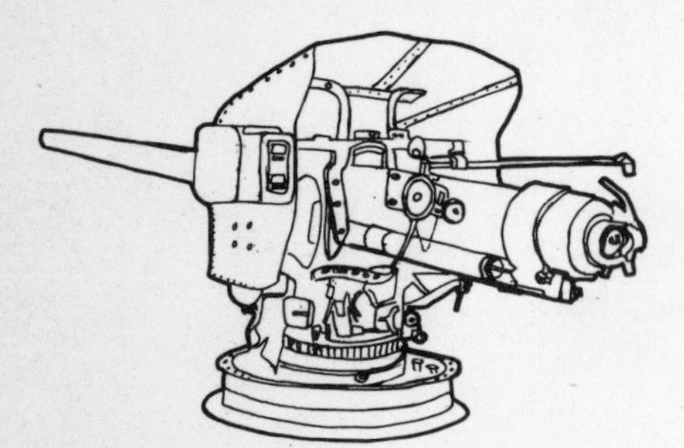

4-INCH NAVAL GUN
In RCN minesweepers, corvettes, frigates and destroyers the 4-inch gun was the standard weapon for surface action. The 4-inch fired semi-armour piercing, high explosive and star shells and had a range of 8 miles.

TAKE IT OFF

A Broadway musical of several seasons ago concerned itself with a burlesque troupe's attempt to give a show in an army camp. According to the story, when the OC heard there was a strip tease involved in the proceedings he called the show off. The burlesque manager's defence was ingenious.

"Isn't it true," he pointed out, "that one of the things the army is fighting for is to defend womanhood?"

"That's true," admitted the Commanding Officer.

"Well, then," retorted the manager, "why in hell don't you let these boys see what they're fighting for?"

Khaki, 1944–1945

Private: "Have you ever been pinched for going too fast?"
Corporal: "No, but I've been slapped."

Khaki, 1944–1945

WALL FLOWERS

Then there was the American soldier who wanted to know about those two girls, EFI and NAAFI, he's hearing so much about.

"Did you tell 'im," says Homer, "that they were two wall flowers accessible to all?"

The Maple Leaf, Italy Edition, 1944

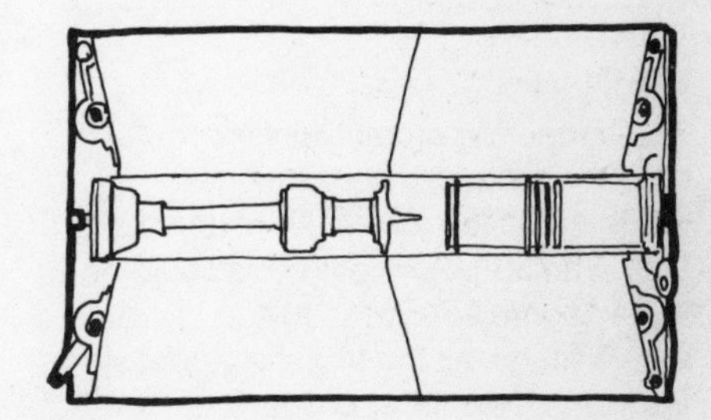

DEPTH CHARGE
Basically the depth charge was a steel cylinder containing approximately 300 pounds of explosives. It could be preset to detonate at depths up to 600 feet. The charges were dropped and fired around the target in a diamond pattern. The explosives were detonated by water pressure activating an explosive primer.

Lipstick adds colour and flavour to a very old pastime.

CWAC News Letter, 1945

Corporal Birkett: "Did you hear the one about the caterpillar with only two hairs?"
McFarlane: "Nope."
Birkett: "He wasn't fuzzy, was he?"

Wings Abroad, 1942

It was noon in the airmen's mess. Orderly Officer McGrath's "Any Complaints" was replied by a shout from Burwash. Walking over he asked, "What's wrong?"

Burwash replied,"What's the idea of this wasp in my soup?"

"That's not a wasp, that's your vitamin B," McGrath answered smilingly.

Wings Abroad, 1942

Hitler was interviewing his troops and stopped to talk to one private.

"How are things with you?" he asked.

"Oh, I can't complain, sir," answered the soldier.

"I'll say you can't," agreed the Fuehrer.

Wings Abroad, 1942

HEDGEHOG
The hedgehog projectile was an electronically fired spigot mortar mounted on the forecastle of an escort ship. The 65-pound projectile could be hurled some 250 yards ahead of the ship. When it hit the target a percussion fuse set off exploder pellets and detonated the bomb.

PUN OF THE WEEK
Why is it dangerous to sleep in a train? 'Cos a train runs over sleepers. Okay—okay.

Wings Abroad, 1941

PUN OF THE WEEK
What did one grain say to the other as they fell down the hen's throat?
We're off to see the gizzard! Well, all right!

Wings Abroad, 1941

CLEAN THOUGHT
One of the best salvage propaganda sign boards in Italy reads: "Get up them stores; but bring back the empties."

The Maple Leaf, Italy Edition, 1944

Front-Line Charlie says: "As a matter of fact I think I *am* eligible for a wound stripe after sitting on that pin cushion at corps."

The Maple Leaf, Italy Edition, 1944

Deputy Minister of Education Rogers recommends no homework for children of sixteen and under. They will then be able to give their undivided attention to the radio.

The Canadian Weekly, 1941

The president of the Shell Oil Company of Canada now rides a bicycle to work. It's a patriotic thing to do, but we bet he always wanted to do it anyway.

The Canadian Weekly, 1941

Goering recently held a reception for his parachute-troops, according to a Berlin social note. But they won't know what a reception really is until they drop in on the British.

The Canadian Weekly, 1941

Manitoba restaurants are making V-Soup by taking the other twenty-five letters out of alphabet-soup. Why don't they save soup by leaving them in and letting them stand for the rest of our war aims?

The Canadian Weekly, 1941

An American tourist at the border last week asked a customs officer if Canadians drive on the left side of the road. No, madam, but some Canadians *lean* to the left.

The Canadian Weekly, 1941

"Joe Moron tied a sand-bag over his tummy because he heard there was going to be a naval bombardment."

TRUCK, 8 CWT., 4 x 4 HEAVY UTILITY CHEVROLET C8A
This type was introduced in 1942 and was manufactured only by General Motors of Canada Ltd. It was used for transporting personnel in small parties and also employed in units as an office vehicle. The rear body could be modified for such roles as ambulance, staff car, wireless and machinery and light repair. All models had an all-steel box-shaped body with side and rear doors. The vehicle had a 6-cylinder in-line 85 hp engine with a 50 mph maximum speed averaging 11 mpg.

London newspapers say the Nazis have built a fake Berlin to mislead the RAF. A secondary purpose is said to be to provide Goebbels with an atmosphere in which he can really think.

The Canadian Weekly, 1941

INCREASED COST OF DYING
The statisticians' latest promulgation—Cost of killing an enemy soldier in the time of Julius Caesar, 85 cents; in Wellington's wars, four dollars and ninety cents. Hang on to your hat, Mr. Taxpayer—the cost per R.I.P. in the present scuffle will most likely run around ten thousand dollars per.

Wings Abroad, 1941

Rumour has it that Ted Yeagar may some day die of lint on the heart from chewing the rag too much.

Wings Abroad, 1941

HOTCHKISS MACHINE GUN
The British Hotchkiss light machine gun was used for anti-aircraft defence and mounted in ships. It was an air-cooled, gas-operated gun firing .303 cartridges and was fed by tempered metal strips holding 30 rounds.

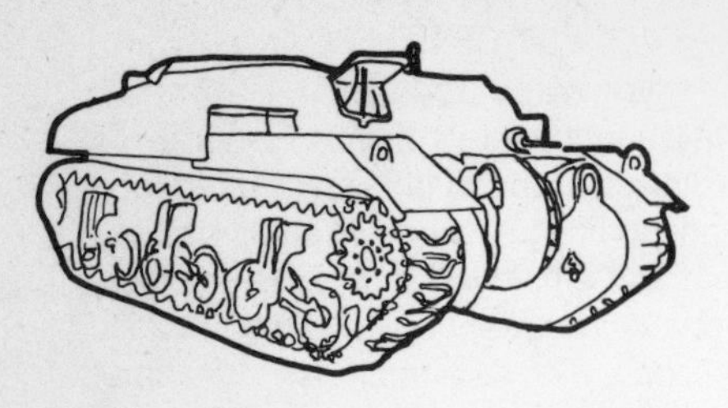

KANGAROO
The Kangaroo was the brainchild of Lt. Gen. Guy Simonds, commander of the 2nd Canadian Corps in the summer of 1944. Simond's armored personnal carrier was made by "unfrocking" some American-made self-propelled guns called Priests. The 105-mm guns were removed and armour plate welded over the openings. Each Kangaroo carried 11 infantrymen plus its crew.

Mayotte: "What did one little strawberry say to the other little strawberry?"
Swain: "Dunno. What?"
Mayotte: "Oh, look at the jam pop got himself into."

Wings Abroad, 1941

THAT WILL BE THE DAY WHEN—
—They find out who left the lit cigarette butt in the local bus, causing the company to lose half its fleet.
—We get paid for our last trade test.
—We get our back rum ration all at once.
—The pup that runs in and out the ranks during parades bites an airman.
—The person who designed the sidewalks and roadways on the camp has to get somewhere in a hurry.
—The little man with the ladder and the blow-torch doesn't have to thaw the outdoor plumbing when Jack Frost pays a visit.

Wings Abroad, 1941

Dear Old Lady: "Little boy, does your mother know that you smoke?"
Youngster: "Listen, lady, does your husband know that you speak to strange men on the street?"

Wings Abroad, 1941

Front-Line Charlie says: "Hand me that extra suit of undies; I'm going up to watch our forward infantry on the ranges today."

The Maple Leaf, Italy Edition, 1944

AVRO LANCASTER
Avro Lancaster B1 heavy bomber was the most successful bomber of the war. Despite its size and power, it handled almost like a fighter. It was all-metal stressed-skin construction. Maximum speed 275 mph at 15,500 feet. Nine .303 guns and a bombload of 14,000-22,000 pounds could be carried. More than 400 Lancasters were built in Canada.

HMMMMMMM!!!!
An MP stopped a pretty CWAC one day after she had passed a group of second lieutenants. "Why didn't you salute those officers, kid?" enquired the military cop.

The CWAC stared at him a moment before replying. Then: "Would you have saluted if they had called you "Toots"?

Khaki, 1944–1945

SPEED
A few years ago the air forces were rushing men through training. One day in a pre-flight class, a student dropped his pencil. He bent down to pick it up and then turned to the man next to him and whispered: "Hey, what did the instructor say?"

"What did he say?" the other one gasped. "Ye Gods, fellow, you just missed a year of solid geometry!"

Khaki, 1944–1945

QUICK REPLY
Then there's the story of the soldier who went into a crowded Montreal restaurant. The waitress asked him for his order.

"I feel like a sandwich," said the Joe.

"Just give me your order please," snapped the girl. "Don't blame me if the place is crowded."

Khaki, 1944–1945

DISCIPLINE
A sergeant returned from Australia tells this one; he saw a kangaroo bouncing down the road with Baby in the front pouch. Every once in a while she stopped and scratched violently. Finally she looked down and came to a sudden stop. She yanked Kangaroo out and began to spank him.

"There!" she exclaimed as she put the squalling brat back. "That'll teach you not to eat crackers in bed!"

Khaki, 1944–1945

A sensible girl is not as sensible as she looks, because a sensible girl has more sense than to look sensible.

CWAC News Letter, 1945

A stolen page from Sergeant Hutch's diary follows:—
7 a.m. to 10 a.m.—I arose (I think).
10 to 12 noon.—Thought.
12 to 1 p.m.—Lunch and breakfast.
2 to 5 p.m.—Will this day never end?

Wings Abroad, 1941

TRENCH TALK
"...and I volunteered to go out on patrol again tonight... there's more cognac where this came from..."

The Maple Leaf, Italy Edition, 1944

Joe Leppington: "Sergeant Albert is pounding away at his typewriter again."
Steve Steeves: "Gee, I didn't know that he could type."
Joe Leppington: "Who said anything about typing?"

Wings Abroad, 1941

A gelding is a stallion with its tonsils out so that he would have more time to himself.

The Beaver Quill, 1942

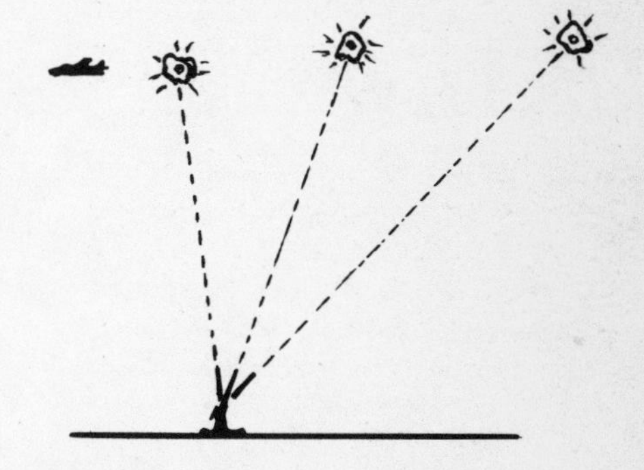

ANTI-AIRCRAFT CEILINGS
The difference between Maximum, Practical and Effective ceilings is shown above: The Maximum, in this case 30,000 feet is that which the shell reaches against the pull of gravity; the Practical, 25,000 feet is that which the shell reaches at the longest setting of the fuse; and the Effective, approximately 18,000 feet is that ceiling at which it is possible to engage an aircraft.

AVRO ANSON
The Avro Anson or "Faithful Annie" was used as reconnaissance plane and a trainer to school navigators, bomb-aimers, and gunners. Canada built Ansons redesigned to take the U.S.-built Jacobs engine. The plane had a maximum speed of 188 mph at 7,000 feet (Mark I). It had a fabric-covered metal fuselage but construction varied.

DAFFY DEFINITIONS
Politician—One who stands for what he thinks the voters will fall for.
Political Bedfellows—Those who like the same bunk.
Bloc—A minority group often led by a blockhead.
Committee—A group of men who keep minutes and waste hours.
Good Speech—An address with a good beginning and a good ending, kept very close together.
Mugwump—A man sitting on a political fence with his mug on one side and his wump on the other.
Taxation—The art of picking the goose so as to secure the greatest amount of feathers with the least amount of squawking.

Wings Abroad, 1941

Front-Line Charlie says: "Was way up today, arranged a correspondence course with educational services."

The Maple Leaf, Italy Edition, 1944

Famous saying in HQ:
"May we quote you on that?"
"Now, wait a minute."

The Beaver Quill, 1941

Two Germans were discussing their vacation plans after the war. One said, "I'll buy a bike and make a tour of Greater Germany." The other, a bit surprised at his friend's peculiar idea, replied, "Good idea, chum, but what do you plan to do with your time in the afternoon, shoot flies?"

The Beaver Quill, 1941

HEARD THIS ONE?
Orderly Officer: "Any complaints today?"
Private Scott: "Yes sir".
Orderly Officer: "What's the trouble my good fellow. Is the meat tough?"
Private Scott: "No sir, the meat is OK. But I can't cut the blasted gravy."

The Beaver Quill, 1941

Said the mama cannon to the papa cannon… "Dear, I think we are going to have a BB."

The Beaver Quill, 1941

The Boss: "Are you a good secretary?"
She: "I don't know, I haven't had mush experience."

The Beaver Quill, 1942

Front-Line Charlie says: "If I wasn't so security-minded I'd tell you more about practising wet landings with EFI for the second front."

The Maple Leaf, Italy Edition, 1944

AT LAST
A private was paraded to his OC and requested a forty-eight hour pass. When asked for a reason he replied that his wife had just been made a RSM in the CWAC

"That's all very fine," remarked the officer, "but why should that get you a forty-eight ?"

"Sir," replied the soldier earnestly,"I want to do something that every private has dreamed of doing for the past hundred years."

Khaki, 1943–1944

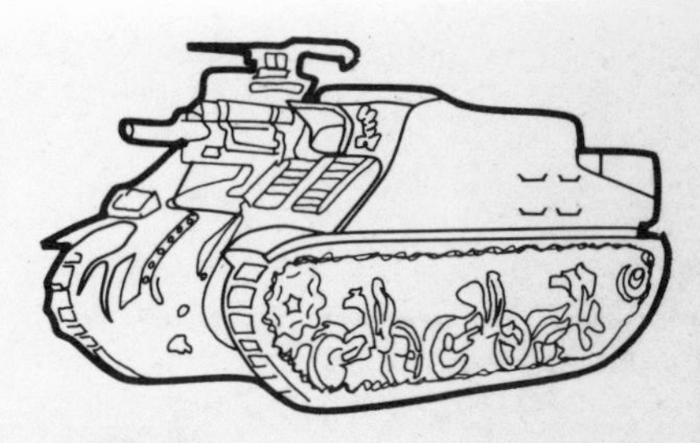

THE PRIEST
The American Gun Motor Carriage 105-mm Howitzer M7 was nick-named the Priest by the British because of its pulpit-like machine gun mounting. It was manned by a crew of seven. The 105-mm Howitzer fired a 33-pound high-explosive shell up to 11,500 yards. It could also be used against tanks. The Priest had a top speed of 25 mph

UNCERTAIN
The lieutenant was going her rounds at breakfast and stopped at one table with the query: "Any complaints?"

One CWAC sprang up and said, "Yes, Ma'am, this tea tastes like chloride of lime."

The officer took the cup, sniffed the contents, then sipped delicately.

"Nonsense," she pronounced. "That's carbolic acid."

Khaki, 1943–1944

DOUBT
The orderly knocked on the captain's door.

"Excuse me, sir, but someone wants you on the phone—I think."

"What do you mean, you think? Don't you know?"

"Well," replied the private, "she said: 'Is that you, you sweet old idiot?'"

Khaki, 1943–1944

A SLIGHT MISUNDERSTANDING
A young Scottish recruit had been placed on sentry duty outside the colonel's tent. Next morning the colonel popped his head out and asked in a stern, loud voice: "Who are you?"

The soldier turned smartly and saluted,"Fine, sirr," he replied, "Hoo's yerse'lf?"

Khaki, 1943–1944

Lieutenant: "Is that your cigarette butt on the floor, Sergeant?"
Sergeant: "It's yours, Sir, if you want it; you saw it first."

CWAC News Letter, 1945

Two chaps were talking about the possibilities of using horse meat in sausages.

First Chap: "Did you ever eat horse meat in sausages?"

Second Chap: "No—and I wouldn't. I had a pal in the last war who was eating sausages made of horse meat and just as he was swallowing someone shouted 'Whoa'—and he choked to death."

Wings Abroad, 1941

LAST WILL AND TESTAMENT OF ADOLF HITLER
Alias ADOLPH SCHICKLEGRUBER
Germany's Public Enemy No. 1.
The Mad Dog of Europe

CERTAIN that my end is near—that is the last fight, and that right must always conquer might—that I have now gone too far.

I GIVE and bequeath all my German people that believe in me to the Dump Friends League.

I BEQUEATH all my medals to Goering, the weight of which together with his own, will bring him to his knees.

I BEQUEATH "Mein Kampf" to Colney Hatch for investigation.

I LEAVE to Goebbels my stock of castor oil, to carry on the traditional work of purges.

I RETURN my moustache to Charlie Chaplin from whom I annexed it.

I BEQUEATH to Ribbentrop my chamber which he may use by raising his right hand in the customary manner.

ON MY DEATH I proclaim the annexation of Hell which I have tried to give my German people and rightfully belongs to the Fatherland.

I APPOINT Ribbentrop and Goering to be executors of this, my Will as they are well experienced in executions.

KNOWING my ultimate destination, I wish to be buried in an asbestos suit.

SIGNED with the left arm upraised.

ADOLPH (The Painter)
Wings Abroad, 1941

OERLIKON 20-MM CANNON
The Oerlikon was mounted in all types of vessels from coastal craft to battle ships. It was an automatic cannon designed for high-angle, close range anti-aircraft fire. It was fed by a 60-round drum magazine firing explosive bullets.

TRENCH TALK

"...and it was so quiet ya coulda heered a grenade pin drop."

The Maple Leaf, Italy Edition, 1944

Very popular this season are girls with blue eyes and green backs.

The Beret, 1946

Sergeant Joe Brown must have had himself a LEAVE. We attribute the present daze to those past days.

OFF THE RECORD

The boy and girl were sitting in the park when a little bug landed on the boy's knee. "What kind of a bug, is that?" the girl asked.

"Why that's a lady bug," was the retort.

"My you have got good eyes, haven't you?" exclaimed the startled girl.

The "Big 2" Bugle, 1944

OFF THE RECORD

"Bloomberg, my neighbour, must be a very wealthy man. He saves $500 a day."

"Five hundred a day! How can he do it?"

"He goes to work every day on the subway. There's a big sign, $500 if you spit. So Bloomberg doesn't spit."

The "Big 2" Bugle, 1944

Cpl. Lewis: "She sure is a striking beauty."
Pte. Edminstone: "You said it - she slapped me twice."

OFF THE RECORD

A private in an army chapel was seen to bow slightly whenever the name of Satan was mentioned. One day the chaplain met him and asked him to explain.

"Well," replied the private, "politeness costs nothing—and you never know."

The "Big 2" Bugle, 1944

EARLIEST BARBER STORY

Q.—"How shall I cut it?"
A.—"In silence."

The "Big 2" Bugle, 1944

Overheard in BOSCOMBE GARDENS: "Let's wait till tomorrow. I don't believe in hasty marriages."

The "Big 2" Bugle, 1944

Run into the roundhouse, Susie. He can't corner you there.

The Beret, 1946

While a Padre was on leave a wandering evangelist obtained permission from the Commanding Officer to address the battalion.

He began with a large distribution of tracts, after which the battalion exhibited the Christian virtues of patience and forbearance for forty-five minutes.

"And now," he said at last, opening his suitcase, "I have a further supply of tracts…" He waited in vain for someone to volunteer as usher and distribute them. "What shall I do with them."

The Commanding Officer spoke up at once. "Ten days CB," he shouted, "for any man who answers that question aloud!"

The Beaver Quill, 1943

LEE ENFIELD RIFLE NO. 4, MARK I

The number 4 was made in Canada and designated Mark I. It carried two 5-round clips of .303 ammunition and it was effective up to 900 yards. A trained man could fire 10 rounds per minute. The Lee Enfield could also launch a grenade from a discharger. Almost a million Lee enfields were manufactured in Canada during the war.

THINGS WE WOULD LIKE TO KNOW

Who was the lady who wrote the authorities asking if it would be possible for her husband to have a "rebore" at Shaughnessy Hospital.

The Beaver Quill, 1942

Front-Line Charlie says: "Ya gotta get forward to get things. Here, see this Luger… only two quid."

The Maple Leaf, Italy Edition, 1944

"Gracie, what's this check stub, one pullover, $25? I don't want to sound like a cheapskate, but isn't that a lot of money for a pullover?"

"The man on the motorcycle said it was the regular price."

"You got it from a man on the motorcycle?"

"Yes, I went through a red light and he drove up and said, 'Pull over!'"

The Beaver Quill, 1942

According to postcards received: The Isle of Wight contains Needles you can't thread, Cowes you can't milk, Freshwater you can't drink, Newport you can't bottle, a Lake you can motor on and a Ryde where you have to walk.

Wings Abroad, 1941

OFF THE RECORD

Mother: "What is this I hear about you petting with your boy friend, daughter? Why when I was a girl we never even dreamt about holding a boy's hand."

Daughter: "Gosh, Mom, they sure musta got away with murder."

The "Big 2" Bugle, 1944

OFF THE RECORD

She decided her nerves weren't so good as they might be and went to a famous Harley Street physician.

He asked her: "Are you troubled by…er…impure thoughts?"

"Oh, no doctor," she replied. "I rather enjoy them."

The "Big 2" Bugle, 1944

FAMOUS LAST WORDS

"Peut-on entrer?"… which in English is… "May I come in?"

The "Big 2" Bugle, 1944

OFF THE RECORD

"Johnny, do you know who built the Ark?"

"Naw."

"Correct for once in your life!"

The "Big 2" Bugle, 1944

The old ladies tell us that a modest girl never pursues a man. Well neither does a mousetrap pursue a mouse.

CWAC News Letter, 1945

Dominion Air Minister Hon. C.G. Powers announces Canada becoming fourth air power of world, outstripping States in producing crews.

Wings Abroad, 1941

TRUCK, 8 CWT., 4 x 2 FORD F8
This vehicle was not used in any active theatre, but was used in the U.K. in limited numbers for carrying supplies and stores and as a general purpose load carrier by Canadian Reinforcement Units. The body was steel welded with hinged tailgate. The average fuel consumption was 13 mpg with a maximum speed of 50 mph It had an 8-cylinder 4-cycle V-8 engine.

The dear old lady approached the bed where a soldier lay almost hidden in a mass of bandages.

"Oh, poor man," she said, "have you been wounded?"

"Oh, no, mum, I bin kicked by a canary."

Wings Abroad, 1941

A little German boy always came and knelt by his father's knee before going to bed. At the closing of his prayers he would always say:—
"Thank God and bless Hitler."

One night 400 Squadron (????) visited Berchtesgaden. Now the little boy just says "Thank God."

Wings Abroad, 1941

HAWKER HURRICANE
Designed in 1934 by Sydney Camm, the Hurricane was the RAF's first monoplane fighter. Some 1,400 were built in Canada. The Hurricane fought also as a fighter bomber and ground attack plane serving on every front. It was of metal airframe construction with metal-covered wings and fabric covered fuselage. Maximum speed (Mark I) 316 mph at 17,000 feet. It had eight .303 guns.

"Say! They're really taking a serious view of this war back home," remarked LAC Campbell, trying on a new pair of running shoes his wife sent him.

Wings Abroad, 1941

Women are trying out shoes with "illuminated" plastic heels, the creation of two St. Louis inventors. The heels are hollow and either transparent or opaque when clear and glittering in gay jewel tones the heels look as if illuminated from within. Some fun in the black out, eh Boys?

Wings Abroad, 1941

A private, passing a second lieutenant, forgot to salute. The lieutenant called him back, commanded him to stand at attention and salute 150 times.

"Just a minute," said a major who had witnessed the exhibition. "Don't you know that every salute should be returned? Get going lieutenant."

When the major departed, the shave-tail had reeled off about 20 snappy salutes, the private counting out loud.

The Tank, 1943

A certain soldier received a ten-day furlough so he could get married and go on his honeymoon. On the eve of the tenth day he wired his commanding officer:

"It is wonderful here. Request ten days extension of leave."

The commanding officer replies: "It's wonderful anywhere. Extension refused. Return at once."

The Tank, 1943

A sailor in a K. of C. hut was heard to make the statement that Canadian minesweepers were very unseaworthy in any kind of a rough sea. He said that in a recent storm, one he was on turned completely over for ten minutes and then righted herself.

RCNMR, 1942

(A letter from Sydney). "The King's wife is in Sydney, too, saw her for the first time last night. Had on a nice grey dress, too, although the ornaments on her rear were rather warlike."

RCNMR, 1942

LAFF O' THE WEEK
Camp Stewart
Every soldier visiting the WAC Detachment here Christmas Day was searched. If he had a piece of mistletoe it was OK. If he didn't possess any, he was led into the day room where "excuses" were hung at six-inch intervals.

The Bullet, 1944

Rest Camp Talk: "...but when she tries to sell me the Coliseum I figger she's been around more'n I thought."

The Maple Leaf, Italy Edition, 1944

A woman leafing through Dorothy Parker's *Enough Rope* at the Public Library last week found this remark penciled in a feminine hand under the crack about men seldom making passes at girls who wear glasses: That's what *she* thinks!"

The Beaten Zone, 1945–46

The most efficient water power in the world is a woman's tears.

The Beaten Zone, 1945–46

Privilege leave on the continent is still in force. You must have an address to go to, and take your own rations.

The Beaten Zone, 1945–46

A hick town is one where there is no place to go where you shouldn't be.

The Beaten Zone, 1945–46

Hello, Mabel, this is Joe. Will you be free tonight? No, Joe, but I'll be reasonable!...

The Beaten Zone, 1945

Man in flower shop: "I want something to go with a weak alibi."

The Beaten Zone, 1945

FAMOUS LAST WORDS
"It must be safe, the BOR is here."

The "Big 2" Bugle, 1944

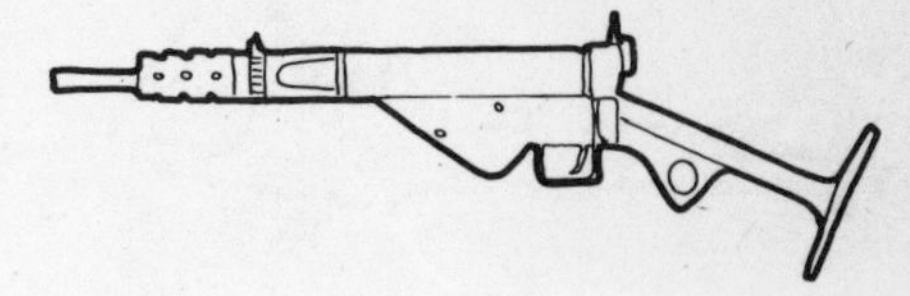

STEN 9-MM SUBMACHINE GUN
Canadians first used the Sten at Dieppe. The Sten was very simple to manufacture. It had only 47 parts, it weighed $9^1/_2$ pounds, had a 32-round magazine and used 9-mm ammunition. Its range was 200 yards and it could fire single or automatic bursts. The gun could be used with a silencer. The name Sten is a combination of its designers Sheppard and Turpin with the first two letters of Enfield the British arsenal. Production cost was approximately $9.00 per gun.

TRUCK, 3 TON, 4 x 4 FORD
The sketch shows the ambulance model, one of the several versions of the heavy utility trucks built on coup chassis. This vehicle was 19 ft. long and $7^1/_2$ feet wide with a house type body 10 feet long. It had room for 4 stretchers or 10 sitting cases. This type of unit was used by RCAMC to transport wounded between field dressing stations, casualty clearing stations and hospitals. The average fuel consumption was 7 mpg and the maximum speed was 50 mph

AIRMEN'S MESS

Yesterday at noon, found hanging on the door of the mess hall, was a placard neatly printed and reading thusly:
Queue,
Stew?
Phew!

Wings Abroad, 1941

DE HAVILLAND MOTH
The Canadian built de Havilland Tiger Moth 82C was a two-seat elementary trainer. It was of wood and metal construction with fabric covering. The maximum speed was 109 mph at 1000 feet. Canada built some 2000 Moths.

It happened at a bomber station somewhere in England. Airman, 'phoning the flight commander: "I have loaded your aircraft with 250's ready for 12 p.m."

"Is that pukka gen?"

"No," said the armourer, "this is LAC White."

Wings Abroad, 1941

WISHFUL THINKING

Since Japan has entered this little "do" we are in, the boys have been indulging in a little wishful thinking about going to Canada to defend its shores. Some even go so far as to say Winnipeg needs us, others say Hamilton, Toronto, and one piped up, "How about Grimsby?"

Wings Abroad, 1942

IT ACTUALLY HAPPENED

Three airmen stepped into the street car in Glasgow. LAC Bone paid his fare with a ticket. Sergeant Thompson paid his fare with a transfer. The third airman walked right by. The conductor called him back.

"Say, you forgot to pay your fare."

"No I didn't" was the reply. "My name is Crime, and Crime doesn't pay."

Wings Abroad, 1942

GREASE MONKEYS

At the Eighth Army health exhibit a New Zealand staff sergeant gathered his audience around a model grease pit beside an ablution table.

"If any of you," he said, "are unfortunate enough to be on fatigue duty that requires cleaning out one of these grease pits here's how to do it..."

At the time his audience comprised three captains, two lieutenants and four sergeant majors!

The Maple Leaf, Italy Edition, 1944

"My sergeant says I'm a first class idiot. I wonder if that is better than a second lieutenant."

RIGHT WORD

A very much-in-love soldier drifted into a Halifax telegraph office and sent a telegram to his one and only in Vancouver. After much pencil chewing and head scratching he finally wrote the following: "I love you, I love you, I love you, Harry."

The clerk read the message over, counted the words and said: "You're able to have another word for the same price."

The Joe thought about it for a few minutes. Then he added the tenth word.

It was: "Regards".

Khaki, 1943–1944

A report from India details the following procedure:
First month: You look under your cot for a snake.
Second month: You look under your cot for a CWAC.
Third month: You look under yourself for a cot.

Khaki, 1943–1944

A soldier, well-known for this stinginess, went into a sea-food restaurant and ordered lobster. He got one that had a single claw.

"What happened to this lobster?" he asked the waiter.

"Must have been in a fight with another lobster and lost his claw," the waiter replied.

"Then why didn't I get the winner?"

Khaki, 1943–1944

A soldier had been calling on a girl for several months. One evening her father popped the question:

"Look here, young man", he said. "You've been courting my daughter for some time now—what are your intentions? Honourable or otherwise?"

The Joe's face lit up. "You mean I've got a choice?"

Khaki, 1944-1945

There was a girl known to her intimates as "BACON"... somebody was always bringing her home.

The Beret, 1946

BEAUTY ABROAD

The streets of Rome
Are paved,
Indeed,
With belles of ev'ry
Race and
Creed.

LORRY, GS, 15 CWT., 4 x 2 DODGE
The Dodge 15 cwt. was a Canadian-built vehicle used by the Canadian Army but was supplied in larger numbers to the British Army and the free French and other allied armies. The body was all steel, with the cab roof removable for shipping and/or operating. The vehicle was 16 ft. 9 in. long and 7 ft. 1 in. wide. It had a 6-cylinder 95-hp engine.

6-POUNDER ANTI-TANK GUN
In 1942 the 6-pounder became the main anti-tank gun of Canada's infantry uinits, and was also used by anti-tank regiments. The 6-pounder had an effective range of 1000 yards. It was usually towed by a Universal Carrier and sometimes by a Ram tank with the turret removed.

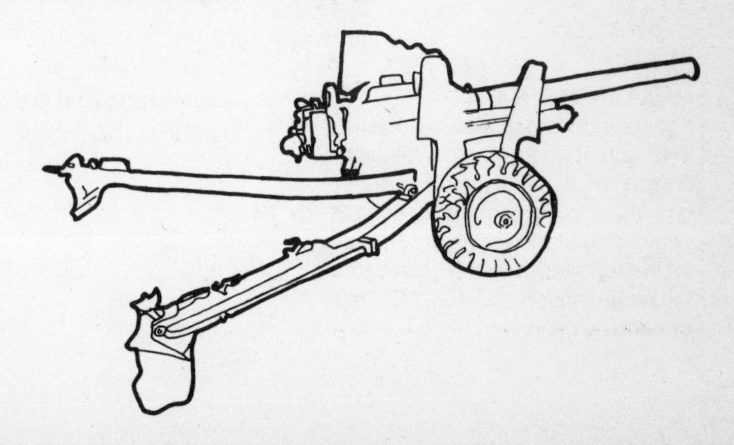

But just today
I saw a
Beauty—
An ATS out
Here on
Duty.

Though Roman gals
Are molta
Bella,
They don't compare
With Private
Stella.

The Maple Leaf, Italy Edition, 1944

HAUNTING PHRASE
The war at long last was over,
The ship steamed for Canada's shores;
When land loomed up over the skyline
The HEAVENS were rent with roars.

The Maple Leaf, Italy Edition, 1944

Front-Line Charlie says: "Was way up today. Took Florence—to the opera."

The Maple Leaf, Italy Edition, 1944

A bubble bath in barracks
Or a mug of beer in Rome.
To drift in peace to Paradise
There's no place like foam.

CWAC News Letter, 1945

In "Ye Olde Days" people were content to wait days for a stage coach. Now they squawk if they miss a section of a revolving door.

Wings Abroad, 1941

Smile—F/S Benson—If a speaker doesn't strike oil in five minutes he should stop boring.

Wings Abroad, 1941

Attributed to a movie critic—"First they had slides, then came movies, then they made them talk—now this one stinks!"

Wings Abroad, 1941

HAWKER TYPHOON
Four Canadian squadrons flew the Typhoon. It was a single-seat fighter-bomber of all-metal stressed-skin construction. Armament varied to 2000-pound bombloads or eight 60-pound rocket missiles to four 20-mm cannon. Maximum speed was 404-413 mph depending on variant.

Noticed on our travels: A sign bearing these words—
"By order of the District Board, cows grazing by the roadside or riding bicycles on the sidewalks is hereby forbidden in this area." Tandem or single?

Wings Abroad, 1941

Then there's the story about the airman who imbibed so frequently that when he died they poured him back into the bottle.

Wings Abroad, 1941

A lady went into a store to purchase some soap. There was an American behind the counter.
Lady: "Have you any lifebuoy?"
Clerk: "Yes, lady. Just set the pace."

Wings Abroad, 1941

ADVICE TO LONESOME LASSIES
Don't envy the gal with wolves at her feet,
Don't sit by yourself and groan.
Bring out your charms you've hidden, my sweet,
And go get some wolves of your own.

The Beret, 1946

OFF THE RECORD
Of a pilot who shot down nine planes in the Pacific, "He certainly hit the Jap pot!!"

The "Big 2" Bugle, 1944

LAFF O' THE WEEK
Two 12-year-old boys paddled their canvas canoe up to a troop ship anchored near an Australian city and asked the goldbraided officer learning over the rail for permission to come aboard.

"No," the officer said, "get out of here."

"Are you the officer of this ship?" asked the small fry in the stern of the canoe.

"No," said the braid, "but I'm the fourth officer.

"Then you'd better learn to be more respectful to your superior officers," the kid replied."I'm the captain of this one."

The Bullet, 1944

LIFE SAVERS
Take good care of the tools and equipment issued to you. An entrenching tool can save your life as well as a rifle.

The Bullet, 1944

SPOTTING THE CONVOY BY DAYLIGHT.

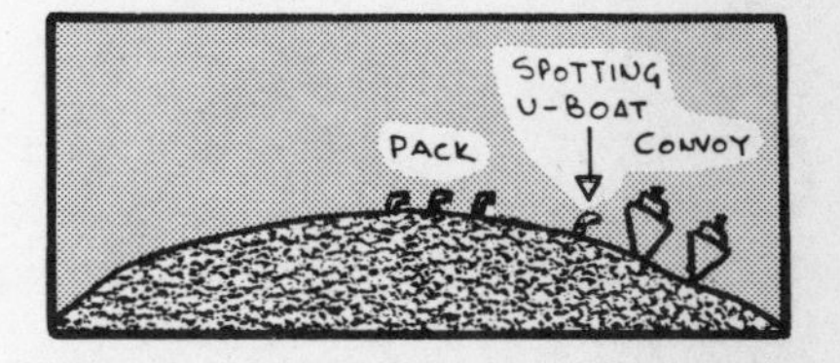

CLOSING IN FOR THE ATTACK BY NIGHT.

METHOD OF SHADOWING A CONVOY
The method of shadowing is for the pack to trail behind or on the flank of the convoy, keeping always just below the horizon and from time to time sending ahead one or more submarines to spot and verify the course and speed of the convoy, and then drop back again.

THAT WILL BE THE DAY WHEN—
We miss the great black cat that prowls around the mess and they serve us furry meat pies.
They stop serving us buckshot for peas.
We get all those parcels that were sent to us last year.

Wings Abroad, 1941

Prophylactic means to bear young in large numbers; a rabbit is said to be prophylactic.

The Beaver Quill, April 1942

If love is blind
And lovers can't see
Then why in hell
Doesn't someone love me?

The Beret, 1946

TRUCK, 15 CWT., 4 x 2 WATER TANKER CHEVROLET
This unit was equipped with a 200-gallon steel tank, power take-off pump, filter unit, suction base, water testing equipment and emergency hand pumps. It was used for pickup, filtration and transporting of drinking water for units in the field. Maximum speed was 46 mph and the average fuel consumption was 13 mpg. Power was provided by a 4-cycle 6-cylinder in-line engine.

CLASSROOM BONERS
—A skeleton is a man with his inside out and his outside off.
—A spinster is a bachelor's wife.
—Celibacy is a disease of the brain.
—An epidemic is a needle the doctor uses to put medicine in your arm.
—Etiquette is little things you do that you don't want to do.
—Shakespeare was born in the year 1564, supposedly on his birthday.
—Robert Louis Stevenson got married and went on his honeymoon. It was then he wrote "Travels with a Donkey."
—An active verb shows action and a passive verb shows passion.
—Milton wrote "Paradise Lost"; then his wife died and he wrote "Paradise Regained."
—Harold mustarded his men before the Battle of Hastings.
—A mountain range is a cooking stove used at high altitudes.

The Beret, 1946

Mikey: "Kin Oi have some…"
Pat (his father): "Here now! Ye've a plate full av food before ye?"
Mikey: "Yis, but…"
Pat: "Well thin, kape yer mout shut an' ate it."

The Beret, 1946

THE STOIC
It was a phony adventurer-soldier who was talking. "This war," he said, "is nothing compared to the one I fought against the Zulus. One of them threw a spear at me and for three days I was pinned to the ground."

"Didn't it hurt?" he was asked.

"Only when I laughed."

The Beret, 1946

TYPE 36 GRENADE
The grenade was a very effective infantry weapon in assaults on pillboxes, machine gun nests and small concentrations of troops. The type 36 could either be thrown by hand or fired from a rifle. The grenade is filled with a high explosive and detonated by a fuse ignited by a cartridge cap. The case of the grenade can break up to 80 pieces, producing a lethal shrapnel effect.

Front-Line Charlie says: "Was way up this week. Carried a small pack off the boat for a CWAC."

The Maple Leaf, Italy Edition, 1944

SLIT TRENCH TALK
"They tell me a Canadian infantry brigade taking part in the Normandy landings donned a Red Patch to instil the fear of the Almighty into Jerry."

The Maple Leaf, Italy Edition, 1944

The following paragraph is an excerpt taken from a letter recently mailed to this headquarters by one of the local units:

"Private Paulsen F. has now been held in custody since the 1st October 1042, and if his documents have gone overseas, may we be advised as soon as this has been ascertained."
Minute 1.
Probably took his documents with him to the Tower of London directly after the Battle of Hastings.

The Beaver Quill, 1942

Hy: "I just found out who the father of all these corny jokes is."
Cy: "Yeah, who?"
Hy: "Pop corn."

The Beaver Quill, 1942

THERE ARE FILES THAT MAKE ME HAPPY
THERE ARE FILES THAT MAKE ME GAY
BUT THE FILES THAT GET MY NANNY
ARE THE FILES I P.A.!!!!!
(Apologies to numerous songwriters.)

The Beaver Quill, 1942

BROWNING GUN
The anti-aircraft model of the Browning was widely used in merchant ships and coastal craft. The gun was water-cooled and belt-fed with a rate of fire of 400 rounds per minute. It fired .50 cartridges.

Famous Last Words: "Nonsense, they're only porpoises."

MAP READING COMMON-SENSE DEFINITIONS

Grid—a self-conscious smile when you have a cold; as in the sentence "grid and bear it." This explains why "grid" and "bearings" are so often mentioned together.

Bearing—the reason you grid. Also refers to the process of having children; but we don't talk about that.

Pass—what CMSC personnel make when they get sitting next to an attractive blonde. Or brunette, We ain't proud.

Contour—what CWACs have, i.e., one of the things they have. The reason why girls wear sweaters.

The Beaver Quill, 1942

CAR, HEAVY DUTY, 4 x 2 FORD
This vehicle was basically a commercial type with only small changes made for military use. Fittings included roll-up black-out blinds, first aid kit, heavy duty tires, strengthened fenders, water and petrol cans and tools. It could carry up to six passengers plus the driver and was used mainly by HQ staff in all kinds of formation. Maximum speed was 70 mph and the average fuel consumption was 13 mpg.

AGE CANNOT STALE HER INFINITE VARIETY

(Telegram from Cairo to a New York Distillery). "Our order 2000 "Old Log" whiskey, ship in transit, affix label our name without mentioning age, Rush."

RCNMR, 1942

Extract from the report of an attack on a submarine, the result of which was not entirely satisfactory to the commanding officer: "After the action, the engineer officer looked at the calendar in his cabin, which has a proverb for each day of the year. He was informed: 'Today thou shalt not slay thine enemy.' The engineer officer has been ordered to destroy his calendar."

RCNMR, 1942

Singeing the King of Spain's beard or Hitler's hirsute horror:
It's all the same:—

A BURNT SHIP

Out of a fired ship, which, by no way
But drowning, could be rescued from the flame,
Some men leap'd forth, and ever as they came
Neere the foes ships, did by their shot decay;
So all were lost, which in the ship were found,
They in the sea being burnt, they in the burnt ship drown'd

John Donne
(Written at the time of the attack on Cadiz, 1596.)
RCNMR, 1942

With tears in her eyes the girl faced her father.

"And when you refused Jack your permission to marry me," she sobbed, "did he go down on his knees?"

Father picked up the newspaper he had been reading before the interruption.

"I don't know," he said firmly. "I didn't notice how he landed."

The Column Courier, 1944–1945

Front-Line Charlie says: "Was way up this week. Wuz knocked on the noggin by a softball at the Corps final."

The Maple Leaf, Italy Edition, 1944

End of a report from a junior billeting officer to his CO: "I was unable, however, to find on the map a small village called "Tenez la Gauche.""

Wings Abroad, 1941

Hitler: "I wouldn't vote for you if you were St. Peter himself."
Churchill: "If I were St. Peter, you couldn't vote for me. You wouldn't be in my district."

Wings Abroad, 1942

Every columnist seems to try his hand in one form of another at picking winners—either along the sport line, politics or what have you: Never let it be said that I didn't get my five cents worth in—I say that Italy will be out of this war by Easter.

Wings Abroad, 1942

A Surrey man claims to have caught a rat with two tails. That's nothing; we're after one with a small moustache!!—Punch.

Wings Abroad, 1941

Among those called up for service was a young welder. For a trade test he was told to make a joint in a piece of steel. When he had finished, the examiner wrote on the man's report:

"Joint very nicely done."

A few days later the recruit found himself posted as head cook in the airmen's mess.

Wings Abroad, 1941

Front-Line Charlie says: "D-Day must have been tough. I remember when I was at CRU and watched the boys come back from 'Tiger'."

The Maple Leaf, Italy Edition, 1944

PAT AND MIKE

It's the cosmopolitan Eighth. A jeep jumped along the main road. On its windshield was the inscription: "Erin Go Bragh." Riding in it were two Indian soldiers.

The Maple Leaf, Italy Edition, 1944

Caption under a topical cartoon: "Mama, what was spaghetti before it was dead?"

The Maple Leaf, Italy Edition, 1944

Homer READ somewhere two lunatics spotted a shapely nude female. Said one to the other, "Wouldn't she look good in a sweater!"

The Maple Leaf, Italy Edition, 1944

Front-Line Charlie says: "I enjoyed the rest camp very much, but it'll sure be good to get up forward again to the B.S.D."

The Maple Leaf, Italy Edition, 1944

Front-Line Charlie says: "The front's very interesting; worked my way up to the mobile laundry this morning."

The Maple Leaf, Italy Edition, 1944

...and then there was the man that had two sons, one joined the QOR and worked for the RQ—and the other wasn't much good either.

The "Big 2" Bugle, 1944

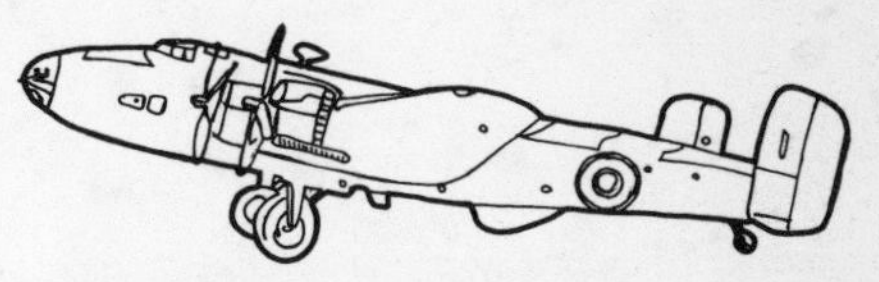

HANDLEY PAGE HALIFAX
First in action in 1941, the "Champ, Big Chief Wa-Hoo, Vicky the Vicious Virgin" names painted on Halifaxes by Canadian crews reflected the affection they felt for the big four-engine bombers. It was also used to tow gliders, to hunt U-boats and to drop agents and arms to resistance groups. The Halifax BII heavy bomber was of all-metal stressed-skin construction. Maximum speed was 280 mph at 13,500 feet. Bomb loads of up to 13,000 pounds could be carried. Armament consisted of nine .303 guns.

25-POUNDER GUN/HOWITZER
From July 1941 the 25-pounder was manufactured in Canada. It was the workhorse of the Commonwealth field artillery units. The gun was effective up to 12,500 yards, with a supercharge up to 13,400 yards. It had a six-man crew and could fire either as a gun or a Howitzer.

LIGHT READING
At the height of the seven-day battle for Ortona a Canadian corporal noticed a Canadian dugout and decided to inspect it. There was nobody about. But on a neatly arranged bed was an open book. The corporal turned it over to examine the title.
The title: "Elements of Crime and Murder."
The Maple Leaf, Italy Edition, 1944

CEMENT MIXER
Someone reported the Germans were putting in concrete fortifications somewhere along the line. Says Homer: "I'll bet a Sherman tank against a grenade pin that the RAF is helping them mix their cement."
The Maple Leaf, Italy Edition, 1944

MOTIVE?
We question the girl's motives. Maybe she is full of honorable intentions, but her motives are under question because of the souvenir for which she has asked her boyfriend, who is fighting in Italy. "Send me part of a bullet that just misses you," she wrote from Canada. Sweet thing.
The Maple Leaf, Italy Edition, 1944

ENGINEERS' BIBLE
They talk of K.R. Can. as the barrack room lawyer's bible. We were a bit surprised this week to learn that for a group of engineers their bible is actually The Bible. The group of Canadian sappers make good use if it, too. Recently they looked for a suitable warning to place in a field strewn with German mines. Their choice: "Ponder the path of thy feet and let all thy ways be established. Turn not to the right hand nor to the left. Remove thy feet from evil."
—Proverbs, Chap. IV, verses 26 and 27…
The Maple Leaf, Italy Edition, 1944

SURPRISE
A soldier home on furlough was having an argument with his wife. After a particularly rough remark from him she burst into tears and said: "How can you treat me like this when I've given you the seven best years of my life!"
Her husband's jaw dropped. "Good Lord," he gasped, "were those your best!"
Khaki, 1944–1945

LIFE SAVERS
Don't let your shadow disclose your concealment. Keep in the shadow and move as its position changes during the day.
The Bullet, 1944

LAFF O' THE WEEK
It was the raw recruit's first turn of sentry duty. So his voice was rather shaky as he exclaimed:

"Halt! Who goes there?"

Out of the darkness came the startling reply: "Foe"

"Have a heart, chum," the sentry protested. "I haven't had time to learn the answer to that one yet."

The Bullet, 1944

SOME LICKING
Germans issue stamps to celebrate friendship of Axis dictators. Anyway, they're in for good licking.

The Bullet, 1944

REVENGE
A soldier in England was known for his loyalty to his fiancee. One day he received a letter from her advising that she was marrying a category "E" gent and would he please return her picture.

His pals were so enraged at this treachery that they rallied to his defence. Collecting photographs, snapshots and pin-up girls from everyone at the camp, they packed them in a huge crate and shipped to the double-crossing girl.

Upon opening the crate she found a note reading: "Please pick out your picture and return the rest to me. This is a little embarrassing but I can't remember which is yours."

Khaki, 1944–1945

If you get into an argument, always try to get in the last word first.

The Tank, 1943

I heard of one man, who after he looked at the income tax schedule, said he either wanted a wife or a cut in wages.

The Tank, 1943

We will never get into trouble hoarding Victory Bonds.

The Tank , 1943

Sarge: "My wife treats me like a stranger."
Corporal: "Well, if she treats you like she treats some of the strangers I've seen her with you shouldn't kick."

Chins Up
Khaki, 1944–1945

Suggestion made by civilian, Sudbury, Ont.—"Why not make puttees thicker on the inside so a soldier's legs will look straighter?"

The Tank, 1940

FIELD ARTILLERY TRACTOR, 4 x 4 FORD
These Canadian-built vehicles were based on Ford and Chevrolet chassis having an all-steel body with a roof hatch for observation. Camouflage, wire and spare tire were carried on the rear of body on top of equipment and tool compartments. The unit was used to tow field artillery pieces and to transport gun crews by RCA field artillery regiments. Maximum speed was 46 mph and the average fuel consumption was 7 mpg. It was powered by a 4-cycle, 8-cylinder, V8 engine.

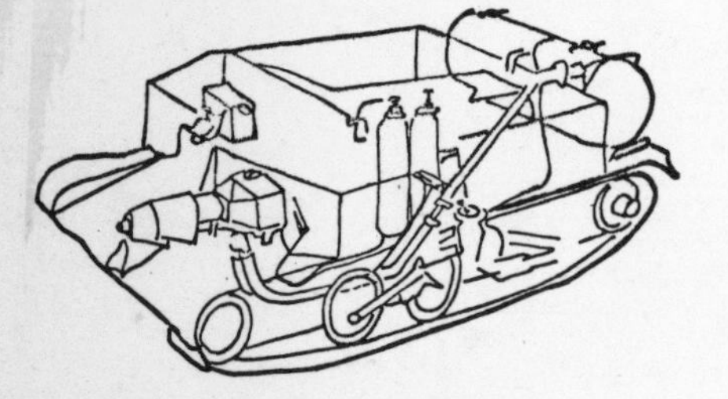

WASP FLAMETHROWER
The Wasp flamethrower was a modification of the Universal Carrier. It had an 80-gallon tank of "fras" (jellied petroleum) propelled to the target by nitrogen gas under pressure through a projector. The Wasp could fire single short shots or a long stream of flame. It had a three-man crew.

A young candidate for the navy was being examined by a Board of Admirals. One of the questions fired at him was:

"What kind of animals eat grass?"

No reply.

"Surely you can answer a simple question like that," snapped one of the admirals. "Now, then, what kind of animals eat grass?"

"Oh, animals," said the candidate, in obvious relief. "I thought you said 'admirals'."

The Tank, 1940

Christian Science is when they cure you and you aren't even there by thinking good things about you even if there aren't any.

The Beaver Quill, 1942

FURLOUGH FAREWELL
I held her tight.
We said: "Good-bye."
We swore Our love would never die.
And then she left me...
What a shame!
—I wish the Hell I knew her name!

Khaki, 1943

PRIVATE COMPLAINT
Lives there a Sarge with nose so red,
Who never in a bar has said:
Hie!
Don' min' if I do...

Khaki, 1943

WE ARE CANADIANS.
We come from the hills, the mountains and the valleys,
We are Canucks, don't you see,
We come from the east, we come from the west,
We come from the land of the free (Gor Blimey).
Chorus—
Now that we're here, with the rest of Britain's sons,
We don't give a damn for Hitler and his Huns.
C—A—N—A—D—I—A—N—S
We are———— We are ————
We are Canadians ————Whoops Gor-Blimey
What do you think of that.

Wings Abroad, 1941

Airman 110: "Hey, waiter? You've just given me a wet plate!"
London waiter: "A wet plate? Why, that's your soup."

Wings Abroad, 1941

That guy with the paint brush has been at it again. On a steep downgrade leading to the Netauro the Provost Corps waxed humorous by posting the sign: "Drive CAREFULLY if you want to see Vienna."

The Maple Leaf, Italy Edition, 1944

The old maid said, "Don't put 'MISS' on my tombstone when I'm dead. I haven't missed as much as you think."

The Beret, 1946

Overheard during the tourist season in Victoria.

"Say, Dad, what's the big V sign for?"

Fond Pa: "Why that's the V for Victory sign. I don't know why they have it blinking all the time, though.

The Beaver Quill, 1941

CANADA'S SHIPBUILDING RECORD

Delivered to end of February 1943:

Type of vessel	**No.**
Frigates	28
Singlescrew corvettes	104
Steel minesweepers	92
Wooden minesweepers	34
Fairmiles	78
10,000-ton cargo vessels	234
4,700-ton cargo vessels	15

Scheduled for 1944:

Type of vessel	**No.**
Frigates	44
Singlescrew corvettes	18
Steel minesweepers	29
Wooden minesweepers	45
Fairmiles	11
10,000-ton cargo vessels	102
4,700-ton cargo vessels	18

GEORGE CROSS
The George Cross was instituted in1940 by King George VI and is the second highest Comonwealth award for bravery. Civilians of either sex are eligible, as are members of the services. The medal is a plain silver cross with a representation of Saint George in the centre slaying the dragon with the words "For Gallantry." It is suspended from a garter blue ribbon.

Couple from south of the border, standing in front of the Victoria Memorial in Parliament Square:
1st Elderly Lady (reading): "Victoria, R.I.—What's the R.I. stand for?"
2nd Lady: "Why Royal Ighness of course, they always drop their H's."

The Beaver Quill, 1941

When we moved into our new house the owner promised us we wouldn't find a single termite. He was right they were all married with large families.

The Beaver Quill, 1941

When a modern bachelor walks the floor with a baby he is usually trying to sober her up.

The Beaver Quill, 1941

THAT'S RIGHT...YOUR'E WRONG
Corporal Squires and Lance Corporal Pashley do not work in the CMSC Orderly Room...We'll say they don't.

The Beaver Quill, 1941

Front-Line Charlie, back from being *slightly* A.W.L., says: "Figure on going way up soon. Is Florence still out of bounds?"

The Maple Leaf, Italy Edition, 1944

We've often heard the airman boast about his ability to spiel off a fifteen or twenty page letter to his girl friend. Here's a little item that will make that fella seem like an illiterate: An Elizabethan courtier wrote a love letter to his lady; it runs to 400 closely written pages and contains 410,000 words! The letter is preserved in the British Museum.

Wings Abroad, 1941

An airman on a long convalescence in a hospital claims that the BBC played "you'd be far better off in a Home" for him every day.

Wings Abroad, 1941

RHYME TIME
It seems an Italian fascist approached a German soldier and asked him for a match. The light was forthcoming.
Said the Itie: "Grazie, Nazi."
Said the Hun: "Prego, Dago."

The Maple Leaf, Italy Edition, 1944

Famous Last Words: "It is O.K. it is just one of ours."

"Have you heard what Hitler's folks said the day he was born? They didn't say anything—they just wagged their tails!"—Walter Winchell.

Wings Abroad, 1941

The story is the one about the woman interviewing an applicant for a maid's job—a girl recently arrived from Europe—and asking her if she could cook, clean, do laundry work, to all of which the applicant answered no. Finally, in despair, the housewife inquired:

"Well, what can you do?"

"I can assemble a machine gun," was the prompt reply.

Wings Abroad, 1941

LIFE SAVERS

Tell the girls nothing except how pretty they are. That's all they should be interested in anyway. One might be a blonde from Berlin.

The Bullet, 1944

One Seaman: "What's that wiggling object on the horizon?
Two Seaman: "Must be a nervous wreck"

What's the matter, Honey. Don't you trust me?"
"Yes, dear, I trust you and I trust me, but I don't trust both of us together."

CWAC News Letter, 1945

Captain: "I demand a high standard of efficiency of my stenographer. Letters going out of this office must be perfect—is your punctuation good, Corporal?"
CWAC Corporal: "Certainly, Sir. I've never been late for duty in my life."

CWAC News Letter, 1945

Little Willie, dressed in sashes,
Fell into the fire and was burned to ashes
Later on the room grew chilly,
But no-one had the heart to poke poor Willie.

CWAC News Letter, 1945

"Haven't I seen that face somewhere before?"
"No, I'm afraid not, I'm the only one that's ever worn it."

CWAC News Letter, 1945

The intelligent girl knows how to refuse a kiss without being deprived of it.

CWAC News Letter, 1945

CONFUSION

"Confusion of Battle" wasn't his sermon theme, but the padre's effort illustrated more than anything the confusion of battle. It was just after his unit, a French-speaking regiment, did its job on the Hitler Line and the padre decided it was time to hold the weekly church service. Not until the service was over did he realize it was Saturday and not Sunday.

The Maple Leaf, Italy Edition, 1944

LUGER LUGGIN LUDWIG

Copies of "Luger Ludwig" have been circulated through brigade and through headquarters of the Canadian 3rd Division. Now they say the British are picking it up. Some call it the "song of the Caen perimeter". Credit for it goes to No.1 Section, D Company, of the Canadian Scottish.

The verses:

Slugging Jerry left and right, having lots of fun, 'til one night,
 we caught him right, now he's on the run.
We licked you on the beaches, chased you through the towns,
 you're not safe if we reach you, so lay that Luger down.
We'll push you across the river and through the fields of grain,
 you'll wish you'd never heard of the Normandy campaign.
We'll blast you in the daytime and muss you up at night, when
 we get through with you, kid, you'll be an awful sight.
Lay that Luger down kid, you haven't got a chance, Luger
 Luggin Ludwig you're all washed up in France.

Khaki, 1944–1945

HOPEFUL

The little private glared at the corporal.

"I feel like telling that corporal where to get off at, again."

The fellow standing next to him sneered. "What do you mean, 'again'?"

"Oh," replied the little guy, "I felt like it yesterday, too."

Khaki, 1944–1945

Moe: "I have a dog and he has no nose."
Greer: "How does he smell?"
Moe: "Awful!!"

The "Big 2" Bugle, 1944

VICTORIA CROSS (VC)
The Victoria Cross was instituted in 1865 by Queen Victoria. It is the highest British Commonwealth award for valour in the presence of the enemy and is open to all ranks of the armed forces. The decoration is bronze, in the form of a Maltese cross, in relief the Royal Crest and bearing on a scroll below the words "For Valour." It is suspended from a crimson ribbon. The VC has been awarded to about 100 Canadians, one-third posthumously, since its institution.

Moe: "I had an uncle with a wooden leg."
Greer: "So what, my mother's got a cedar chest!!"
Moe: "Is that right you were once an actor, Al?"
Greer: "Yeah. I had my leg in a cast!!!"

The "Big 2" Bugle, 1944

OFF THE RECORD
We can say one thing about the Germans: they made us believe things we didn't believe we could believe.

The "Big 2" Bugle, 1944

Heard in "A" Flight Hut: "Open the doors and let some of this smoke out. There's enough smoke in here to smoke a ham, and I'm no ham."

Wings Abroad, 1941

STAGHOUND ARMOURED CAR
The Staghound was used by armoured car and reconnaissance regiments for a variety of functions. Its maximum armor thickness was 1 1/4 inches, could reach speeds up to 55 mph and was manned by a crew of five men. The Staghound was armed with one 37-mm gun and two .30 machine guns.

FAMOUS LAST WORDS
"We don't need smoke, it will be okay."

The "Big 2" Bugle, 1944

OFF THE RECORD
WAAF: "I have a beautiful face, beautiful shoulders, perfect bust and perfect waist—say George Saltstone are you following me?"
CQMS Saltstone: "I'm way ahead of you."

The "Big 2" Bugle, 1944

A soldier just home from the Solomons reports that the mosquitos grow so big out there that one night a refuelling crew put 100 gals of petrol in one before they found out it wasn't a Liberator.

The "Big 2" Bugle, 1944

PRACTICAL
A private strolled into a lunchroom and ordered two sandwiches.
"Will you eat them here or take them out with you?" enquired the waitress.
The Joe looked at her mildly.
"Both," he replied.

Khaki, 1944–1045

Heard in the R.A.P. "Cut off my arms and call me Ampy!"

The "Big 2" Bugle, 1944

"I always think the magazine's the best place for a quiet smoke."

OFF THE RECORD

Waitress: "I have fried liver, boiled tongue, stewed kidneys and pigs' feet."

Moe: "Don't tell me your ailments, sister. I came in for a chicken dinner."

The "Big 2" Bugle, 1944

CSM Chivers, bellowing to a rifleman: "The afternoon off! The afternoon off! What the (censored) do you think you are—a human being?"

The "Big 2" Bugle, 1944

FAMOUS LAST WORDS

"The barrage is over."

The "Big 2" Bugle, 1944

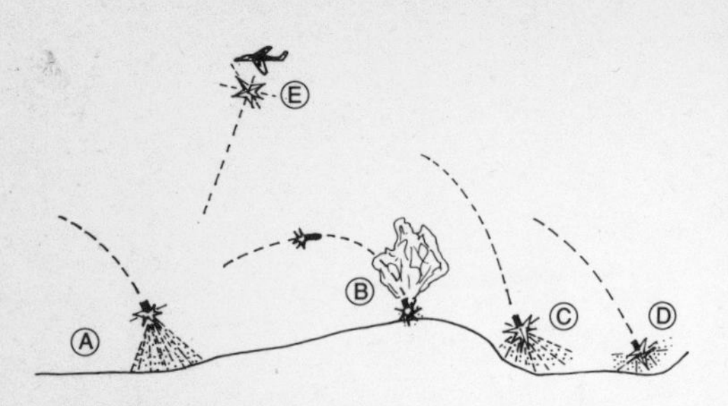

THE ACTION OF SHELLS
A. Shrapnel
B. Impact-fuzed smoke shells
C. Time-fuzed high explosive, using fragments to search out targets behind dead ground
D. Impact-fuzed high explosive
E. Proximity-fuzed high explosive

OFF THE RECORD
For centuries the position of Arab women in North Africa was lowly. When travelling the man always rode the family donkey while the woman carrying the household goods walked behind. But with the coming of war British and American troops, etc., many customs changed. The man still rode the donkey but the woman was emancipated. She walked in front. THERE MIGHT BE LAND MINES!

The "Big 2" Bugle, 1944

FAMOUS LAST WORDS
"Let's go down to "A" Echelon."

The "Big 2" Bugle, 1944

This was heard in the "Naffy" yesterday. Corporal Richardson had been waiting patiently to be served. He wasn't getting any attention so he called the "Naffy" waitress.
"Have you been to the Zoo?" he asked.
"No," replied the waitress.
"Then you ought to go. You will find it very thrilling to watch the turtles rushing past you."

Wings Abroad, 1941

This was overhead on sick parade the other day.
"Now, Harry King, " said Doc Wallace, "what is the matter with you?"
"It's like this doctor," was the doleful answer. "You know how you feel when you don't know how you feel? Well, that's how I feel."

Wings Abroad, 1941

PAY-DAY
Eat, drink and be merry, for tomorrow you will have to scrounge pennies.

Wings Abroad, 1941

"Well," said Sergeant Harling, "there's one thing I can say: I'm a self-made man."
"Are you boasting," inquired MacMillan, "or apologising?"

Wings Abroad, 1941

GUN, HOWITZER AND MORTAR TRAJECTORIES
The gun fires on a flat trajectory, at high velocity for direct shooting at visible targets; the howitzer fires shells at a high angle for indirect shooting; the mortar fires shells at angles over 45°, lobbing them into enemy positions from steep angles.

PUN OF THE WEEK
Knock, Knock!
Who's there?
Quaker Oats.
Quaker Oats who?
Continued next week, it's a Cereal (Serial).
(Well, we thought it was phunny.)

Wings Abroad, 1941

Corporal Kennedy, W/T Section, claims that it is better to give than to lend, and it costs about the same.

Wings Abroad, 1941

The squad of air force recruits had been out to the rifle range for their first try at marksmanship. They knelt at 250 yards and fired. Not a hit. They moved up to 200 yards. Not a hit. They tried at 100 yards. Not a hit.

"Fix bayonets and charge!" ordered the sergeant. "It's your only chance."

Wings Abroad, 1941

A SLIGHT ERROR

A sergeant was trying to teach his charges the difference between right and left. After a hectic half hour he ordered the platoon to raise the right leg. One confused Joe raised his left in error: The NCO looked down the line and saw the upraised left leg right next to the upraised right leg of the recruit beside him. "Hey!" he roared. "Who's the smart aleck in the middle of the line who's got both legs off the ground?"

Khaki, 1943–1944

Famous last words from Moe: "and all I said to the guy was – 'Yeah! You and who else!'"

M.O. "You have acute appendicitis."
C.W.A.C. "Listen Sir, I came here to be examined - not admired."

DEFINITION
The paratroopers are naturally very curious guys. One lad approached his instructor after a lecture and asked: "What happens if, after we jump, the parachute doesn't open?"

The sergeant looked at him for a moment, then replied.

"My boy," he said, "that would be jumping to a conclusion."

Khaki, 1943–1944

CONSOLATION
It was after Church Parade. The padre had held forth violently on the Ten Commandments and Private Glutz was visibly affected. He crawled slowly back to his hut and sat on a bunk, head in hands. Suddenly he looked up with a bright smile on his face.

"Well," he said, "at least I've never made any graven images."

Khaki, 1943–1944

SITUATION WELL IN HAND
During the recent fighting at Ortona, a young soldier suddenly hollered for help.

"What's wrong?" replied a comrade who was patrolling nearby.

"Hurry up," yelled the voice. "I've got six Jerry prisoners here—and they won't let me go."

Khaki, 1943–1944

We heard George Dykes the other morning saying, "This insomnia's got me worried, I can't sleep even when it's time to get up."

Wings Abroad, 1941

Hunter (to old guide): "Have you ever been lost in the woods?"
Old Guide: "Nope—I was bewildered once for four days."

The Column Courier, 1944–1945

A German and a Dutchman met in the street. The German raised his hand and said "Heil Hitler!"

The Dutchman raised his hand and said "Heil Rembrandt!"

"Why Rembrandt?" asked the German.

Replied the Dutchman: "He was *our* best painter."

The Column Courier, 1944–1945

Sandy Saks: "What is your opinion of Hitler's manpower situation?"
Editor: "He's at his Fritz-end."

The Column Courier, 1944–1945

A policeman grabbed a girl in Piccadilly a few nights ago and said: "I'm taking you in charge."

"Fine," said the girl, "I always wanted to work under state control."

The Column Courier, 1944–1945

An American soldier in London was trying to give an Englishman some idea of the size of Texas.

"Why, in Texas you can board a train one morning, ride all day and all night, and the next morning you're still in Texas."

"Really," replied the Englishman. "I thought only our English trains were that slow."

The Column Courier, 1944–1945

"ODE"
I took her to a night club,
I took her to a show,
I took her almost everywhere,
A boy and girl could go.
I took her to dances,
I took her to tea,
And then suddenly I realised
That she'd been taking me.

Wings Abroad, 1941

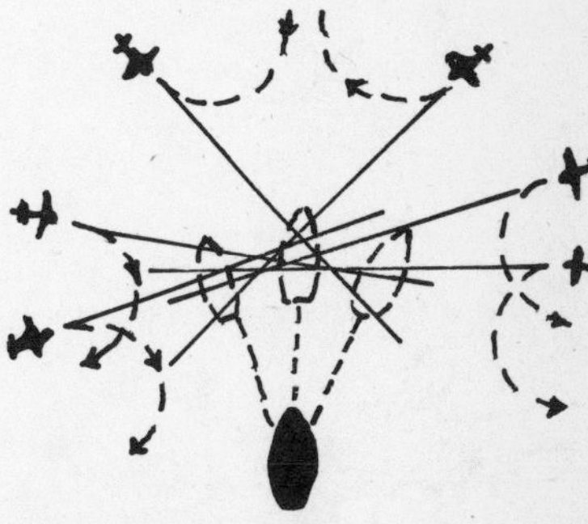

TIN FISH ATTACK
Diagram shows techniques used in attacking one ship or a convoy. Torpedoes are launched so that, no matter what avoiding action the ships take "strikes" would be registered. Aircraft turn away in pairs and resume formation.

Ideas are funny little things. They won't work unless you do.

Wings Abroad, 1941

RECIPE FOR SLIMMING
Doctor: "The best way to slim is to shake the head slowly and deliberately."
Fat man (looking puzzled): "And how often should I do that?"
Doctor: "Each time your friends say 'Have a drink.' "

Wings Abroad, 1941

A little story of a Neutral who was shown over the birth place of Schiller the German poet.

"Here," announced the Nazi's guide, "our national poet was born."

"International," corrected the Neutral, "for he wrote 'Maid of Orleans' for the French, 'Egmont' for the Dutch 'Mary Stuart' for the British."

"Nothing for the Germans?"

"Sure," said the visitor. "He wrote the 'Bandits'."

Wings Abroad, 1941

Johnny Nisbett's new girl friend is so attractive that when he takes her home he can hardly keep his eyes on the meter.

Wings Abroad, 1941

LEWIS MACHINE GUN
The .303 Lewis, used in World War I was Canada's standard light machine gun until it was replaced by the Bren gun in 1939. The rotating gun magazine held 47 rounds, it was gas operated and could be fired only in full automatic. The navy used the Lewis as an anti-aircraft gun.

MORALE
Morale is the making the winning of the war our NUMBER 1 objective.

The Beaver Quill, 1942

Patient: "Doctor, how are my chances?"
Doc: "Oh, pretty good, but I wouldn't start reading any continued stories."

The Beaver Quill, 1941

LIFE SAVERS
Flash lights or matches should never be lighted outdoors at night in a combat area. Such lights serve the enemy as well as a beacon does the pilot.

The Bullet, 1944

Omer: "See that bevy of quail in the underbrush?"
Joe: "Yes,"
Omer: "Well watch me shoot a hole clear through the red barn behind them."

The Beaver Quill, 1941

Customer: "Have you a book called "Man, the Master of Women?"
Salesgirl: "The fiction department is on the other side, madam."

The Beaver Quill, 1941

WHEN DANGER IS NEAR AND WAR IS NIGH
TO GOD AND THE SOLDIER THE PEOPLE ALL FLY.
BUT WHEN WAR IS OVER AND EVERYTHING'S RIGHTED
GOD IS FORGOTTEN AND THE SOLDIER IS SLIGHTED

The Beaver Quill, 1941

SWEET VIOLETS
Just as a gag a brigade major got out an operational order on fly control. Under a heading, "Improper Use of Latrines" he directed:
a) On no account will latrines be used for any other purpose than that intended.
b) Severe disciplinary action will be taken on any personnel using latrines as slit trenches.

The Maple Leaf, Italy Edition, 1944

Steve: "That was a dandy sermon the Padre gave on marriage today."
Moe: "It sure was, and I wish that I knew as little about the subject as he does."

The "Big 2" Bugle, 1944

TRUCK, G.S., 30 CWT., 4 x 4
CMP 4 x 4 types in this class were produced from 1940 to 1943 by General Motors (C30) and Ford (F30) until production was discontinued in the interest of vehicle standardization. The vehicle was used in the United Kingdom by CRV or other base units as a general-purpose load carrier. The body was steel with hinged sides and tailgate, superstructure, tarpaulin, lockers for tools and equipment. Power was supplied by an 85 hp 6-cylinder engine with a maximum speed of 50 mph averaging 9 mpg.

1st CWAC: "She's got the most liquid singing voice."
2nd CWAC: "Well, now that she's pouring it out in the bathtub, I hope it runs out with the water when she pulls the plug."

CWAC News Letter, 1944

Williams Mk. III: "Did you know that the CO is a famous lecturer, I heard him today."
Williams Mk. II: "How come?"
Williams Mk. III: "Oh, I spilled some coffee down his neck at breakfast and he got up and said a few words."

The "Big 2" Bugle, 1944

The other night we heard (via short-wave telegraphy) a Canadian Maiden offering the following prayer, very earnestly and fervently, to the Man Upstairs: "Dear Lord, please bring him back, safe, sound and *single*!"

The "Big 2" Bugle, 1944

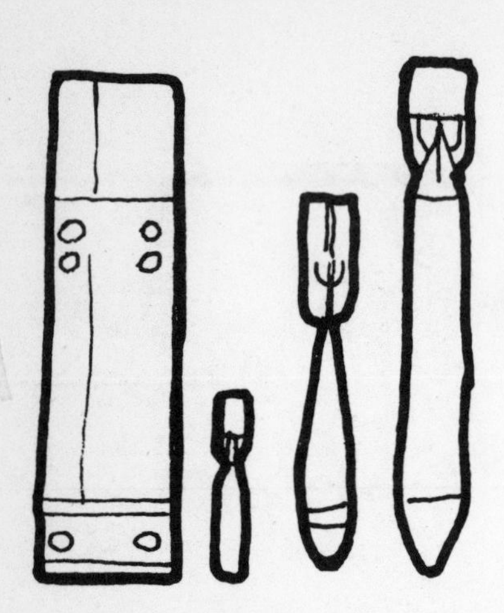

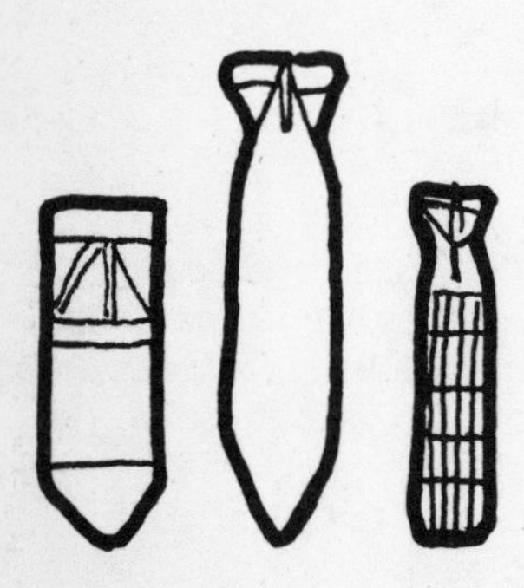

THE BOMBS
Several types of bombs were used by Bomber Command: target indicator bombs to mark the bomb-release point; incendiary bombs to set fire to flammable objects, such as military and other buildings; high explosive GP (general purpose) bombs to effectively destroy buildings, and concentrations of equipment and/or personnel.

...of course you know that life-jackets are called "Mae Wests" but did you hear that the CWACs who came into Normandy re-christened theirs "second fronts"?

The "Big 2" Bugle, 1944

REAL ESTATE
The Canadian reinforcement, just over from Blighty, was looking over a battered old Italian villa, when a veteran of Sicily and Italy approached him. "Thinking of buying the place?" he asked. "Me?" declared the reinforcement, "why I wouldn't want to haunt it!"

The Maple Leaf, Italy Edition, 1944

Scotty Barnes claims that the finest after dinner speech he ever heard was: "Scotty, I'll settle with the waiter."

Wings Abroad, 1941

We heard of a man in town whose wife had nagged him into a nervous breakdown. "What you need, " his doctor told him, "is a good rest."

The patient thought a moment. "I can't afford it, doctor, Would it be alright if I sent my wife to see a double feature at the Regal?"

Wings Abroad, 1940

Report of a monument in France which marks the last resting place of an army mule:
In memory of Maggie who in her time kicked:
2 Colonels
4 Majors
10 Captains
24 Lieutenants
42 Sergeants
432 Other Ranks AND
1 Mills Bomb

Wings Abroad, 1940

New pilot (after Lysander familiarization test): "Say, is the undercarriage retractable on this machine?"
NCO rigger: "Well, yes and no Sir—after that last landing I'm not sure!"

Wings Abroad, 1940

Can someone tell us where the idea originated for heating a room with a basin of hot water? We are informed by a certain person that the results are quite speedy.

Wings Abroad, 1940

A little child, before going to a hospital for an operation, was told by his mother to be a good boy and act like man. The little boy said, "Don't worry, Mom, they ain't going to pan a baby off on me like they did on you—I want a pup."

Wings Abroad, 1940

It's brain food that makes CWACs so intelligent—fish on Fridays and noodle dishes for the rest of the week.

CWAC News Letter, 1944

"A" Squadron Rumour—
"You can't take your girl's picture overseas with you on account of in case you are captured the enemy could get a line on your friends."

The Tank, 1941

In his book, "Through the Dark Night," War Correspondent J.L. Hodson tells of asking an infantry major: "What comforts do the men need most?"
The reply: "The girls they left behind them."

The Tank, 1941

A man has perfected a gadget that provides appropriate smells with talking pictures—*Kitchener Record*. We've had an idea that they've had pictures with smells for a long time.

The Tank, 1941

And then there's the butcher who backed into his slicing machine; thus getting a little behind in his business.

The Tank, 1941

ECONOMY OF AMMUNITION
"Stand behind your lover, false woman," roared the Scotsman, as he caught his wife with the ice-man—
"I'm going to shoot you both!"

The Tank, 1941

Our Adjutant, Capt. Joyce, wishes to say one thing: "Be careful riding those d----- motorcycles."

The Tank, 1941

Arny Robinson's Korny Kernal for the week: "I'm practising cutting my finger nails with my left hand in case my right hand gets shot off."

Wings Abroad, 1941

A Cuckoo is a bird that lays other bird's eggs in its own nest and vice versa.

Wings Abroad, 1940

BLOCKBUSTERS
During the latter part of the war the Allies used demolition bombs such as the 12,000-pound Tallboy and 22,000-pound Grand Slam deep penetration bombs to destroy viaducts and the German Navy's U-boat pens. Demolition bombs that weighed 10,000 pounds or more were commonly called Blockbusters.

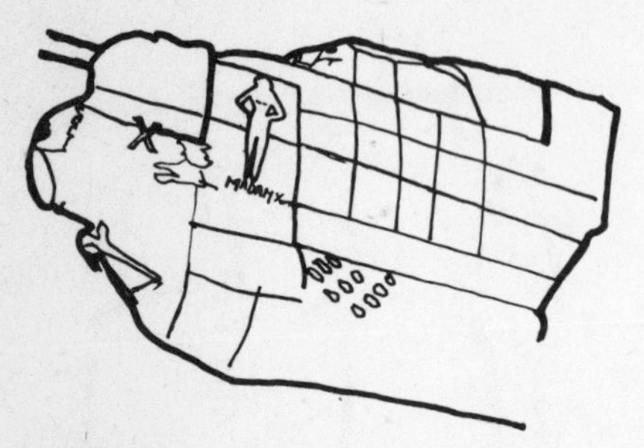

INSIGNIA
In addition to the official insignias and camouflage on aircraft pilots and crews decorated the fuselage with personal unit markings and insignia. Without a doubt the female form was the most popular shape. Some were flamboyant, some saintly and some women of doubtful virtue. Yet, other crews preferred a name instead of an insignia!

THE JEEP
The Jeep became one of the war's best known symbols. It originated from a small runabout designed by the Bantam Car Co. prior to 1939. U.S. Army approved a prototype based on the Bantam and contracts for mass production were give to Willys Overland Co., and later to Ford. It was a 4 x 4 and could do 55 mph. The Jeep was used for countless vital military tasks.

GENUINE INGENUITY

One day, while on camp patrol, an RCAF Service Police was stopped by a new RAF recruit.

Recruit: "Could you direct me to the Watch Office?"

SP: "Yes, but what is the nature of your business at the Watch Office?"

Recruit: "Well, I was told that I could get my watch fixed up, you see the spring is… Etc."

Wings Abroad, 1940

Gilles Fortier was giving a few points to a Frenchman learning English when a Scotsman helpfully intervened:

"Your-r-r-r English is guid, lad, but ye must gao aboot tr-r-ryin' to get the r-r-right accent."

Wings Abroad, 1941

Often heard on the Despatch Office telephone, 1625 hours.

Officer (on wire): "Would you send a truck out to 'C' Flight dispersal to pick me up, please?"

Airman on the wire five minutes later: "Send a truck out to 'C' Flight right away, will yuh!" I've gotta get in for early supper. Haven't had a bite since three p.m. and I'm going out tonight."

Wings Abroad, 1941

Our Sage, "Honest" Bill Copely, says for the book this time: "Repatriation may be the aim of most; but all I want is to be able to spell it.'

Wings Abroad, 1941

1st CWAC: "The kids tell me I talk in my sleep—what shall I do?"

2nd CWAC: "Nothing you shouldn't."

CWAC News Letter, 1944

Sister E: "Gert, get off that man's knee!"

Gert: "Oh Sister! I got here first!"

The Beret, 1946

PLEASANT CONVERSATION

The colonel descended on the company in training.

Colonel: "A nice day today. Very fine weather we are having."

Captain: "We certainly are, Colonel."

Colonel: "It was very fine yesterday."

Captain: "It was."

Colonel: "And the day before was a fine day."

Captain: "Quite so, sir."

Colonel: "Then where did the mud come from on those lorry wheels?"

The Bullet, 1944

EXPLOSIVE

Brown: "So it's all over between you and Violet?"

Jones: "I'm not sure. She's high explosive girl."

Brown: "High explosive—what do you mean by that?"

Jones: "Oh, just dangerous when dropped!"

The Bullet, 1944

A GOOD START

Raw recruit: "If you stood in my shoes, what would you do?"

Sergeant: "I would give them a shine to start with."

The Bullet, 1944

THE LESSER EVIL

Three Canadian airmen, sleeping in a tent in one of the English training areas last summer, were rudely awakened by a terrific crash not far away.

"What was that—thunder or bombs?" asked one.

"Bombs," was the laconic answer.

"Thank heaven for that," chimed in the third. "I thought we were going to have more rain."

The Bullet, 1944

TRENCH TALK

"That war correspondent must be one of the those underground writers you hear about; he types his stuff in a slit trench."

The Maple Leaf, Italy Edition, 1944

MISUNDERSTANDING

Private Murphy had gone home on furlough, and one evening he went off on a party. When he returned home with the key he proceeded to navigate the front hall. Suddenly his progress was halted by a loud crash of broken glass. This awakened his wife, who called down sweetly, "Is that you dear? What happened?"

"It's me alright," replied Murphy, "And that'll teach those goldfish not to snap at me!"

Khaki, 1944–1945

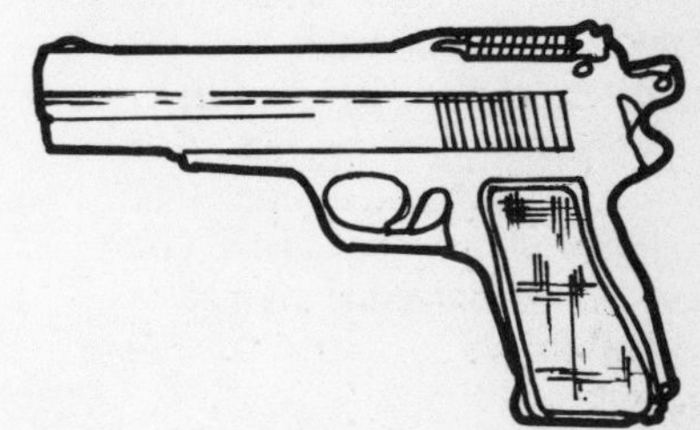

PISTOL, BROWNING (FN) 9MM., HP, NO.2 MK. I

Pistols were mostly used by armoured and airborne troops and by Commando and similar units who specialized in close-quarter fighting. The above model was produced in Canada but without the wooden holster stock and the graduated tangent backsight as in the original design. The Canadian and British version had a simple fixed-backsight. The Browning fired the standard 9-mm cartridge with a magazine capacity of 13 rounds. It was 7.75 in. long and weighed 2 lb, 3 oz. Manufacturer was John Inglis and Company in Toronto.

One morning recently, a young woman
Got out of bed,
Slipped into her robe,
Stepped into her slippers,
Raised the shade,
Uncovered the parrot,
Put on the coffee pot,
Answered the phone.
And heard a masculine voice say:
"Hello, Honey, I just got off the ship and have
24 hours leave. I'm coming right up."
So the lady unlocked the door,
Took off the coffee pot,
Pulled down the shade,
Covered the parrot,
Slipped into bed,
And heard the parrot mumble
"KEE-RIST, WHAT A SHORT DAY!"

The Column Courier, 1944–1945

UNIVERSAL CARRIER
Bren or Universal carrier was the Canadian Army's standard carrier. It was a lightly armoured tracked vehicle carrying four to six soldiers and their weapons. It was also used in many other roles such as carrying wounded men, anti-tank gun, machine gun, ammunition, food and water carrier, and as a headquarters vehicle. Maximum speed was 30 mph and average fuel consumption was 4 mpg. Canada built close to 34,000 Universal Carriers during the war.

LIFE SAVERS
Don't throw or leave boxes, tins, cans, munition cases or any refuse in the open. They should be buried as they indicate activity in the area.

The Bullet, 1944

Baby ear of corn: "Mama, where did I come from?"
Mama ear: "Hush dear, the stalk brought you."

The Beaver Quill, 1941

The working of a Lewis gun is: "The striker pin hitting the base of the cartridge, explodes the charge which forces the cartridge up the barrel followed by spare parts.

Wings Abroad, 1941

A proselyte is a woman of the streets.

The Beaver Quill, 1942

CONFIDENTIALLY
LAC Garard was heard to ask if a sub-lieutenant in the navy is the officer commanding a submarine.

Wings Abroad, 1941

LAC Rollins enquired of McFarlane why aircraft had Artificial Horizons installed instead of real ones. (Maybe they were cheaper).

Wings Abroad, 1941

LAC Sicox wants to know if new pilots use more green flares than experienced ones.

Wings Abroad, 1941

Adult: One who has stopped growing except in the middle.
Willpower: The ability to eat one salted peanut.

Wings Abroad, 1941

And then there's the story about the budding pilot in the Link Trainer who was jolted by the instructor's casual remark, "Incidentally you are flying at an altitude of minus forty feet. What do you think you are, an underground railway?"

Wings Abroad, 1941

The orderly officer happened to be in the cook-house the other day and noticed an airman carrying what appeared to be a large bowl of soup. "Hi there, let me taste that." The airman meekly condescended and gave him a large ladleful. Spluttering and fuming he roared, "Do you call that soup?" The airman humbly replied, "No sir, that's dishwater."

Wings Abroad, 1941

Said one GI to another, "Women like strong silent men because they think they're listening."

CWAC News Letter, 1945

"So you complain about finding sand in the soup, Private Fuzzybie."

"Yes, Ma'am."

"Did you join the army to serve your country or complain about the soup?"

"To serve my country Ma'am—not to eat it."

CWAC News Letter, 1945

Lieutenant: "The CWAC who sneaked out of the barracks last night and met a sailor over by that tree will step forward. Er…um…Platoon, Halt."

CWAC News Letter, 1945

And then there was the sailor who loved so many CWACs it's platoonic!

CWAC News Letter, 1945

Sergeant: "How often have I told you to fall in on parade on time, Corporal?"
Corporal: "I don't know, Sarge. I thought you were keeping score."

CWAC News Letter, 1945

CAR, LIGHT SEDAN, 4 x 2 FORD
Ford Canada produced this type mainly for British use although many were used by the Canadian army for transportation of staff officers. The Canadian-built sedan had right hand drive while the U.S.-built vehicles kept the original left hand drive. The body was sedan type, all-steel, four-door construction seating five including driver. To suit this vehicle for miltary use equipment such as rifle racks, blackout curtains, map container, fire extinguisher and first aid kit was supplied. Average fuel consumption was 14 mpg and the maximum speed was 80 mph

THE VETERANS GUARD OF CANADA
The Veterans Guard of Canada was one of the Legion's great contributions to the war effort. Some 15,000 First War vets served in the VGC, one of the main duties being that of guarding prisoners of war and prison camps.

They say there is no distinction between Capital and Labour in the air force, but we beg to disagree…
The money you lend is Capitalism and getting it back is real Labour.

Wings Abroad, 1941

A man who marries twice commits bigotry.

The Beaver Quill, 1942

FOR YOUR INFORMATION, PLEASE
A good girl always sticks to no;
A bad girl always yesses;
A smart girl makes them sound alike
and holds them all in guesses.

CWAC News Letter, 1945

Could it be that the weaker sex is often the stronger sex because of the weakness of the stronger sex for the weaker sex.

CWAC News Letter, 1945

Girls, if you're wise to Dan Cupid,
He'll settle your life—not up-scoop it.
To be kissed by a fool
Is bad, as a rule;
To be fooled by a kiss is plain stupid.

CWAC News Letter, 1945

Intuition is that gift which enables a sergeant to arrive instantly at an infallible and irrevocable decision without the aid of reason, judgment or discussion.

CWAC News Letter, 1945

"These rations are important," said the Messing Officer, "for the meat of today may be the hash of tomorrow."

CWAC News Letter, 1945

SMILES
She: "Here's your ring back. I cannot marry you, for I love someone else."
He: "Who is he?"
She (nervously): "You're not going to kill him?"
He: "No. But I'll try to sell him the ring."

Wings Abroad, 1941

Women are wiser than men because they know less and understand more.

The Tank, 1943

If fate didn't knock us flat on our backs now and then we might never learn to look up.

The Tank, 1943

We must sail sometimes with the wind, and sometimes against it—but we must sail, and not drift, nor lie at anchor.

The Tank, 1943

Goering wanted more night bombers very urgently. So he went along to a factory.

"I want a dozen of your planes," he ordered. "They must be ready three nights from now."

"Impossible!" exclaimed the works manager.

"I command!" roared Goering. "The crews will be here at the time stated."

At the specified time the crews arrived. German efficiency had triumphed; the planes were ready. Without loss of time they set out for the target—England.

Over London the leading pilot pulled the bomb-release lever—and out dropped three of the factory's night shift.

The Tank, 1943

HOW LARGE WERE THE RATIONS?
$1\frac{1}{3}$ ounces tea, $5\frac{1}{3}$ ounces coffee, $\frac{1}{2}$ pound sugar, and $\frac{1}{2}$ pound of butter each week; one choice twice a month from a wide variety of jams, jellies, honey, marmalade and other spreads for which the rations varied from 6 to 12 fluid ounces; 1 to $2\frac{1}{2}$ pounds meats each week. Automobile owners were entitled to 40 units of gasoline yearly, each unit having a value that varied during the course of the war, for non-essential passenger cars. Owners of essential and commercial vehicles obtained gasoline on the basis of proven individual requirements.

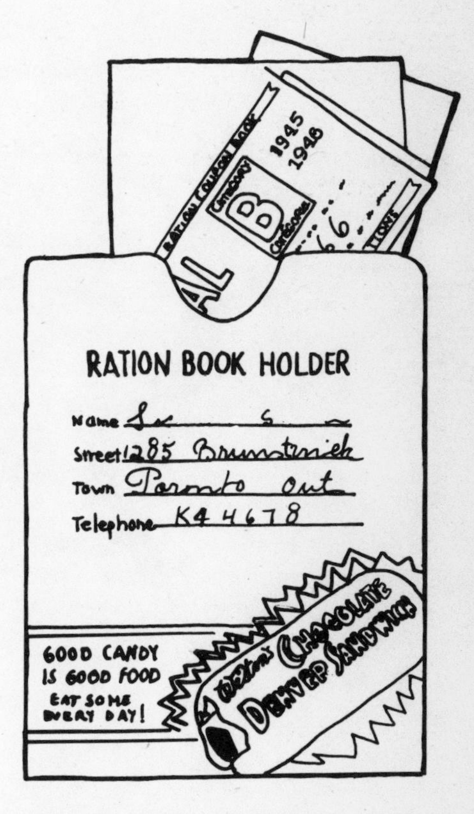

WHAT COMMODITIES WERE RATIONED IN CANADA?
Tea; coffee; sugar; marmalade; jam; jelly; honey; corn syrup, maple syrup, molasses, and maple sugar; canned fruit; butter and meat were rationed. Gasoline was also rationed, and many luxury goods were unobtainable.

A crowd of German airmen arrived at the gates of heaven and clamoured to get in. "Who are you?" asked St. Peter. "We're the fifty German airmen who were shot down today by the RAF," was the reply. Said St. Peter: "Wait a minute while I have a look at the communique." After reading it he came back and announced: "It says here that only two German airmen were shot down today. So two of you can come in and the rest of you can go to hell."

The Tank, 1943

TRIPLE P's
They call them the "Triple P's. Spelled out this stands for "PAUL PINK'S Privies." Lance-Bombardier Paul Pink has a sure-fire idea for construction of latrines. He makes them for an artillery unit from old charge boxes. No comments, please.

The Maple Leaf, Italy Edition, 1944

A private in the garrison is still searching for the key to the parade ground. Finding the rookie gullible, a sergeant detailed him to pick up the mythical key from the company sergeant-major. The CSM informed the private that the key could be found on the last post.

Looking in desperation for the "last post" our hero encountered the RSM. "Sorry you can't pick up the key, lad. We sent the last post to be whitewashed," said the RSM. "Better get back to your platoon."

Khaki, 1943–1944

Rumour has it that the RCA has a new field piece which fires so rapidly that it shoots twelve times before you didn't know it was loaded.

Khaki, 1943–1944

A gunner, home on leave, was sitting with his cat before the fire. His wife had to go and visit some relatives and warned him to keep an eye on the fire. She went out. The gunner fell asleep. Two hours passed. The fire died. The wife returned. She took one look at her husband snoring before the dead fire, and screamed: "FIRE!"

The husband leaped to attention, tore open the door of the oven, rammed in the cat, slammed the door and cried: "Number One gun, Ready Sir."

Khaki, 1943–1944

THOMPSON .45 SUBMACHINE GUN
Canadians used the famous American Thompson. It was used to bolster rifle fire and for special purposes suich as commando and paratroop attacks. The Thompson had a rate of fire of 650 rounds a minute fed from a box or drum magazine.

And not so long ago a soldier returned from overseas was being interviewed on a radio program.

"Were you ever a hero?" he asked.

"Sure," replied the soldier, "I saved my whole regiment once."

"You did?" enquired the interviewer, all suspense. "How?"

"I shot the cook," modestly replied the Joe.

Khaki, 1943–1944

"What is the point in my buying a subscription to 'Wings Abroad'? I can't see any point in it," said one of the three non-subscribers in 400 Canadian Squadron to the circulation manager.

"Well, it will show you how to be a better airman."

"Listen, fella. I'm not half as good an airman as I know how to be."

Wings Abroad, 1941

Corporal Bert Miller recently came to earth like a burned out comet. While on the frosty wing of a "Hurricane" he made an attempt at the world's ski-jumping record. Well, the record still stands but not wee Bertie.

Wings Abroad , 1941

Attributed to Johnny Gair in an unguarded moment of frustration and frigidity while coaxing warmth from his English fireplace—"Many are cold but few are frozen."

Wings Abroad, 1941

Heard around the mess hall since the new rations came out—"Well, if that was my dinner, I guess I've had it."

Wings Abroad, 1941

We have it straight that the big brick building being built on the field is for the express purpose of decontaminating rumours. It will need to be all of that size judging by the way 400 has been rumour-mongering lately.

Wings Abroad, 1941

CANADIAN RED CROSS ASSOCIATION
The Canadian Red Cross Society equipped and built a Canadian military hospital "somewhere in England" at the cost of a million dollars.

CANADIAN RED CROSS
PRISONER-OF-WAR PARCEL
Sample Food Parcel #1: It cost about $2.50 and added to the diet provided in the enemy camps for prisoners of war. Typical contents: 1 box of cheese, 1 tin of salmon, 1 tin of margarine, l packet of chocolate, 1 tin of jam, 1 tin of dried milk, 1 tin of chicken and vegetables, 1/2 pound of sugar, 1 tin of tomato juice, 1 tablet of soap, 1/4 pound of tea, 1 tin of bacon, 1 box of figs, 1 cellar of salt, 1 packet of ginger biscuits and 1 tin of lemonade.

"Biggest issue after the war will probably be who who goes back to the kitchen."

GLOSSARY
For the information and guidance of all those who have recently arrived in this country, the following vest pocket size dictionary has been compiled and is submitted for your approval and whatever action you may deem necessary.
Bloke—screwball.
Blimey—(censored).
Cinema—show.
Flicks—pictures.
Pit—orchestra.
Circle—balcony.
Stalls—gallery.
Sweets—candy.
Sandwich—one half of what you think it is.
Snack bar—dog car.
Queue—line up.
Daft—screwy.
Faswakdkajdfk plifiehgkskal—Fares please!!

Wings Abroad, 1941

Clerk: "Shopping bags?"
Gals: "No, just looking."

The Beret, 1946

LIFE SAVERS
Where you have been or where you might be going is your business, no one else's. The oceans are deep, wide and rough—you can't swim back you know.

The Bullet, 1944

Sergeant Bettridge: "Say Mike, I hear that McCullough got shot by one of the prisoners you were bringing in, didn't you search them for weapons?"
Corporal Overy: "Sure did, but one of them was a girl—and you can't be too thorough with a woman y'know."

The "Big 2" Bugle, 1944

Red Cockburn: "Remember that cheese you served for supper last night?"
Moe: "Yeah."
Red Cockburn: "Did you say that it was imported or deported from Switzerland?"

OFF THE RECORD
Hear about the Big Twoer being shown around one of London's famous buildings?

"Debates have been held here for more than 300 years," said the guide.

"Anything decided yet?" asked the Canuck.

The "Big 2" Bugle, 1944

Moe: "Did you get the job in Battalion HQ?"
McQuade: "Yep!"
Moe: "What're you doing?"
McQuade: "Same as everyone else, nothing!"

The "Big 2" Bugle, 1944

Frank Bowler now claims that, in view of recent events, a three-point landing is "Two wheels and a propeller."

Wings Abroad, 1941

A circle is a line of no depth running round a dot for ever.

The Beaver Quill, 1942

According to the Bible, Job was the most patient man on earth. No wonder, he didn't have to work on aircraft.

Wings Abroad, 1941

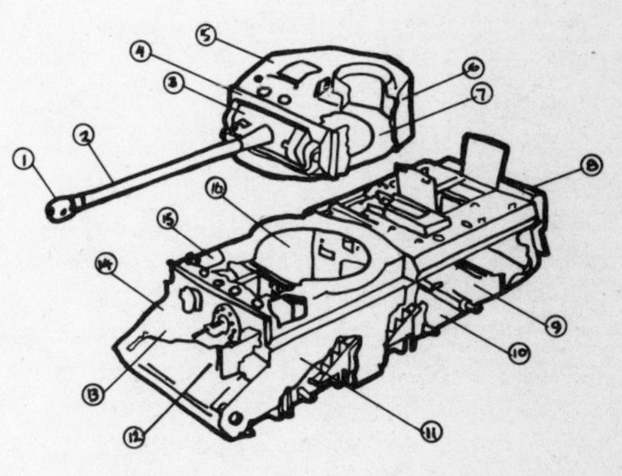

THE PARTS OF A TANK
The above "exploded" view shows some of the more common terms used to describe the general layout of a tank.

1. Muzzle break
2. Tank gun
3. Mantle
4. Turret front plate
5. Turret roof plate
6. Turret side plate
7. Turret base plate
8. Outlet louvres
9. Engine compartment
10. Floor plate
11. Outer side plate
12. Front gunner's compartment
13. Driver compartment
14. Glacis plate
15. Driver's door
16. Fighting compartment

Who's the wise guy when told by the flight sergeant he should have been on parade at 8 o'clock, replied: "Why, what happened?"

Wings Abroad, 1941

It is claimed that it takes twenty to sixty years for the roots of the briar to attain size suitable for pipe making. You would smell too, if you were underground that long.

Wings Abroad, 1941

A martyr is a pile of wood set on fire with a man on top.

The Beaver Quill, 1942

As one rheumatic pain said to the other: "Let's get out of this joint."

Wings Abroad, 1941

25-POUNDER SELF-PROPELLED GUN, SEXTON
The Sexton was built by Montreal Locomotive Works to British specifications. The basis of the design was the chassis of the Ram, having the standard British 25-pounder field howitzer and the British wireless No.19 set. The Sexton had good armour, fire power and cross-country performance. It had a crew of six (commander, driver, gunner, gun-layer, loader and wireless operator). Maximum speed was 25 mph and the road radius approximately 140 miles. The Sexton was in production from 1943 until the end of 1945, by which time over 2100 vehicles had been produced.

"Who was the lad who insisted his rifle 'kicked' when firing a ·22 at the armoury?"

The airman's mess hall "Utopia" has been discovered. A prominent sign reads in part, "Airmen are encouraged to have a second meal."

Wings Abroad, 1941

Civilian onlooker to sergeant, watching manoeuvres.

"That's good training in more ways than one. Those three men over there are supposed to represent a hundred men and that old wheelbarrow a tank. That's real imagination!"

Sergeant: "That's no imagination, damn you—that's stark reality."

The Beaver Quill, 1942

Then there is the story of the Sergeant who dreamed he was lecturing to a platoon of raw recruits...
and woke up to find it was true.

The Beret, 1946

WELL, I'LL BE!...
In his caravan, in a sea of Italian mud and slush Major Jim McAvity, Saint John, N.B., of an armored brigade opened a Christmas parcel which arrived from his brother in the United States the other week. "Well, at last they've come,"he said staring at some items he'd written for while still stationed in Blighty.
—A dozen tennis balls!

The Maple Leaf, Italy Edition, 1944

Homer has a "simply wizard" idea for a gift for mothers-in-law. "Send her an Ortona-Chieti railway ticket," suggests Homer.

The Maple Leaf, Italy Edition, 1944

Front-Line Charlie says: "Was up there again today. Look... got my boots muddy."

The Maple Leaf, Italy Edition 1944

NO SUGAR
The Canadian infantryman lay wounded for more than three days in a swampy gully. Finally, by flashing a mirror he was able to attract the attention of a Canadian patrol. Some men went out after him and brought him back to our lines, where they wrapped him up and brewed a mess of tea.

"Will you have some tea?" they asked this lad who had not eaten or drunk for almost four days.

"Yes," he said, "but no cream or sugar, please."

The Maple Leaf, Italy Edition, 1944

WOTA ANSA!
The above story was told to an ENSA girl. Her only comment was: "My sister doesn't take cream or sugar with her tea either."

The Maple Leaf, Italy Edition, 1944

Irvine: "Oh! by the way, there is a parcel over in the hangar for you."
Prest: "Good! Whom is it from?"
Irvine: "I don't know, but there are cigarettes, gum, cakes and chocolate bars in it."

Wings Abroad, 1941

WRONG NUMBER
The captain was late getting out of camp for his week-end leave, and was very annoyed when a husky, pink-cheeked soldier suddenly blocked his way. "Halt, who goes there?" demanded the guard dutifully.

He was pushed aside in an unmilitary fashion.

"Can't you see I'm your captain, running for the bus?" was the reply as the captain made a dive for the last bus that was closing its doors.

The guard scratched his head for a moment and then called weakly after him: "Pass, Captain Running-for-the-bus."

Khaki, 1944–1945

WHAT IS THE WAR COSTING CANADIANS?
In the fiscal year ended March 31, 1944, it is estimated that the war will cost Canadians more than $13,000,000 each day.

MISUNDERSTANDING
The army has been using mules in Italy, and one day an officer came upon a group of men with an odd assortment of spades, shovels and guns in their hands. He walked up to the leading figure in the group and asked: "Where's that mule I told you to take out and have shod?"

"Yipe! Did you say shod, sir?" stuttered the soldier. "We just buried her with military honours."

Khaki, 1944–1945

Said the bugler upon being personally wakened by his commanding officer:
"Hello, CO,
Guess I'd better blow."

Khaki, 1944–1945

CANADA'S DAILY WAR COST PER PERSON
POPULATION 11,506,655

FAIREY BATTLE
The Fairey Battle was somewhat obsolete by the time the war began. It was designed as a light bomber before the war. A single Rolls-Royce Merlin 1,030 hp engine powered the aircraft. It was armed with a .303 machine gun in one wing and a Vickers K gun in the rear and could carry a 1,000-pound bomb load. Its maximum speed was 241 mph at 13,000 ft and the normal range was 1,050 miles. A total of 2,185 planes was built before production was suspended in 1940. Many Battles were sent from Britain to Canada for use in air gunnery schools.

WAR BIRD
The mischievous stork is a courageous bird. That we know. But so are Canadian infantrymen who helped deliver an Ortona mother of her child at the height of the battle. Members of a Pacific coast highland battalion served as midwives in the midst of heavy shelling and carried out a successful delivery.

Says Homer: "The child, conceived under Fascism, has been delivered in freedom."

The Maple Leaf, Italy Edition, 1944

Rudy Brulé, looking at Alfie's long fangs: "Gee, I'm going to paint this dog black and train him to be a night fighter."

Wings Abroad, 1941

MOTORCYCLE, SOLO HEAVY, HARLEY-DAVIDSON TWIN
Motorcycles were used to provide rapid transportation for despatch riders and other personnel such as the Canadian Provost Corps whose duties required them to move between various operational and non-operational areas. Maximum speed was 60 mph and the average fuel consumption was 35 mpg.

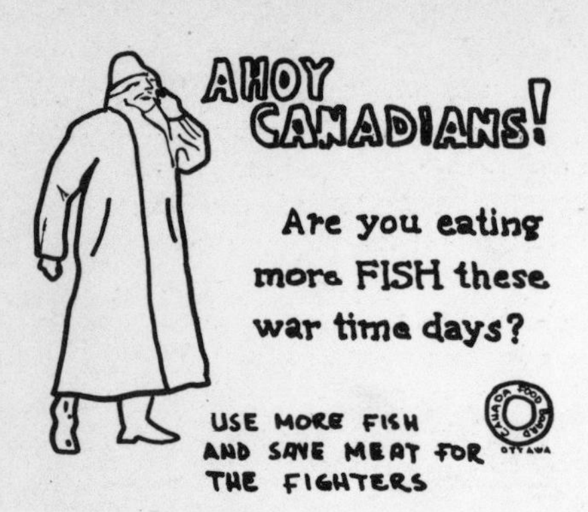

Canadians were great at catching fish but not so great at eating them! During the war years the government tried to encourage Canadians to increase their fish consumption with advertising posters similar to one above produced by the Canada Food Board in Ottawa.

25-POUNDER STAR SHELL

1. Transit plug (removed prior to firing the shell and replaced by a time fuse)
2. Gunpowder burster (to be ignited by the time fuse when the shell was in the required position)
3. Flare or star
4. Cables attaching flare and parachute
5. Parachute
6. Shear pins (holding base plate in position prior to and during firing)
7. Base plate (blown out by burster as parachute and flare were ejected)

Various types of carrier shells were developed for the 25-pounder gun/howitzer from smoke screen to armour-piercing shot.

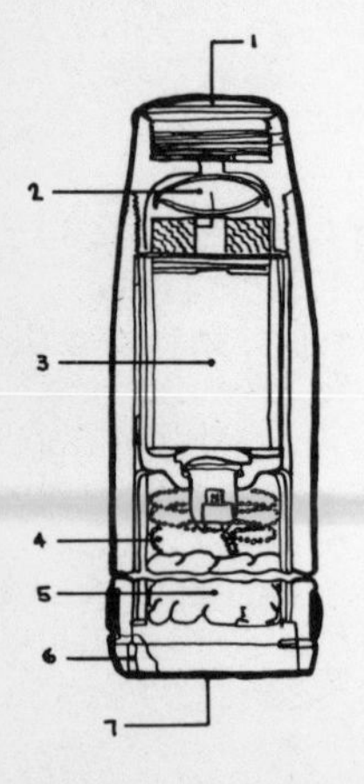

MUST WE MENTION MUSTARD

"Mustard has an almost endless number of strange uses.
1. Keeps mice away.
2. Stimulates egg production in poultry.
3. Keeps pests off the garden.
4. Cleans sink drains.
5. Two ounces stop a car radiator leak.
6. Removes ink stains.
7. Good for dogs with distemper.
8. In paste form will keep loose tiles in place."

Wings Abroad, 1941

Mayotte: "Why did the coal scuttle?"
Swain: "Yuh got me. Why?"
Mayotte: "He saw the kitchen sink."

Wings Abroad, 1941

Edgebert AC3: "Between Admiral Cunningham and our cooks using it for soup the Mediterranean sure is taking a beating."

Wings Abroad, 1941

Jimmy Duval's latest is that an R.C. is one who is to be Repatriated to Canada.

Wings Abroad, 1941

Edgebert, AC3, on visiting village near field: "Nice statue you've got in the square there, but why the funny pose?"
Local Yokel: "Aye, laddie, that monument was meant to be an equestrian statue, but the reeve and council of this hamlet ran out of money before the horse was put under it."

Wings Abroad, 1941

IN AND OUT

Did you ever hear the story of Mrs. Skunk who had two little skunks named IN and OUT. She had a little trouble with them because every time IN was in, OUT was out, and every time IN was out, OUT was in.

One day when IN was out, she sent OUT out to bring IN in. When OUT had brought IN in, she asked him how she did it.

"It was easy," answered OUT. "Instinct".

The Beret, 1946

TALL ORDER

From "Curly" and "Joe" on RMCS *Prince David* comes the following letter just in time to catch the Christmas deadline:

Dear Santa:

We are two lonely sailors far way from home who think we will not be home for Christmas (Editor's Note—Are you kidding?).

We would be obliged if you could send us the following on Christmas night, repeat night:

1. One blonde, 5' 2", eyes of blue.
2. One redhead (brunette will do if the former is not available).
3. Six cases of Johnny Walker's Scotch Whiskey.
4. Ten cases of Black Horse.
5. Three sets of loaded dice.
6. Two discharge papers or a commission.
7. One medal, one mention in dispatches.

Oh Santa, we know you won't let us down.

C. AND J

Trusting fellows, aren't they!

The Maple Leaf, Italy Edition, 1944–1945

CORVETTE

The Corvette was designed by W. Reed of Smith's Dock Co., Yorkshire. It was intended as a coastal escort but was used as an ocean escort providing anti-submarine protection for convoys of merchant ships. The corvette was smaller and more manoeuvrable than a destroyer. Due to its short length of 195–252 feet many were built in small shipyards on the Great Lakes in Collingwood, Kingston, Midland and Port Arthur. Corvettes carried antisubmarine and antiaircraft guns, depth charges, and listening devices to detect submarines. All the Canadian built-units were named for towns and cities. Canada built 106 Flower Class corvettes, *Wetaskiwin* being the first completed of the thirteen west coast-built corvettes.

Front-Line Charlie says: "Was 'way up today—might get three points this month."

The Maple Leaf, Italy Edition, 1944–1945

Water is composed of two gins. Oxygin and Hydrogin. Oxygin is pure gin and Hydrogin is gin and water."

The Beaver Quill, 1942

Orderly officer, inspecting M.Q. barracks: "Who's that chopping wood upstairs?"
Voice upstairs: "No one, sir. It's just me eating the biscuits in my parcel from home."

Wings Abroad, 1941

Chivalry is a man's inclination to defend a woman against every man but himself.

The Beret, 1946

Our Winston Churchill has capitulated and offered Italy half the Mediterranean—the bottom half.

Wings Abroad, 1941

Flight Sergeant Bailey (in bed): "Jerry's over again!"
Sergeant Murphy (also in bed): "Never mind—we'll clean it up in the morning!"

Wings Abroad, 1940

Adolescence is the stage between puberty and adultery.

The Beaver Quill, 1942

I think of you often,
And I write you every day,
But there's so very little,
That seems worthwhile to say.

It either rains or doesn't,
It's either hot or cold,
The news is uninteresting,
Or else it's all been told.

The only thing that matters
Is the fact that you are there,
And I am here without you,
And it's lonesome everywhere.

I think of the way you smile,
And I recall your touch,
And distance lends enchantment,
And I miss you very much.

The Beret, 1946

Enraged father: "I'll teach you to make love to my daughter!"
Soldier: "I wish you would, old man. I'm not making much progress."

The Beret, 1946

The thing about common sense is that it's not common.

The Beret, 1946

CO-ED—A girl who also goes to college.

The Beret, 1946

HERE IS SOME NOOSE
Give a convict enough rope and he'll skip.

The Beret, 1946

The spine is a bunch of bones one on top of the other that keep you from being legs all the way up.

The Beaver Quill, 1942

BATTERIES
Twinkle, twinkle, Little Star,
WHAT the HELL d'you think y'are?
A flashlight?"

The Maple Leaf, Italy Edition, 1944–1945

Front-Line Charlie says: "Was away up yesterday. Went up to hear Seven Solid Senders send salutations to Sinatra."

The Maple Leaf, Italy Edition, 1944–1945

SIXTH SENSE
The thing called intuition is one of those things that is highly underrated according to Corporal Zeke Williams of Edson, Alta. During the "season" when the Canadians were pushing up to the Reno River, Williams was driving Captain D.W. Smilie of Ancaster, Ont., up to their BCD area. The road was under shellfire and, as the closeness of the shelling became closer, the two suddenly decided that it would be much better if they abandoned their vehicle in favour of a ditch. No sooner had they settled down to the comforts of the improvised slit-trench, when a shell scored a direct hit on the vehicle. Both men looked up to see their armored car taking off in all directions.

The Maple Leaf, Italy Edition, 1944–1945

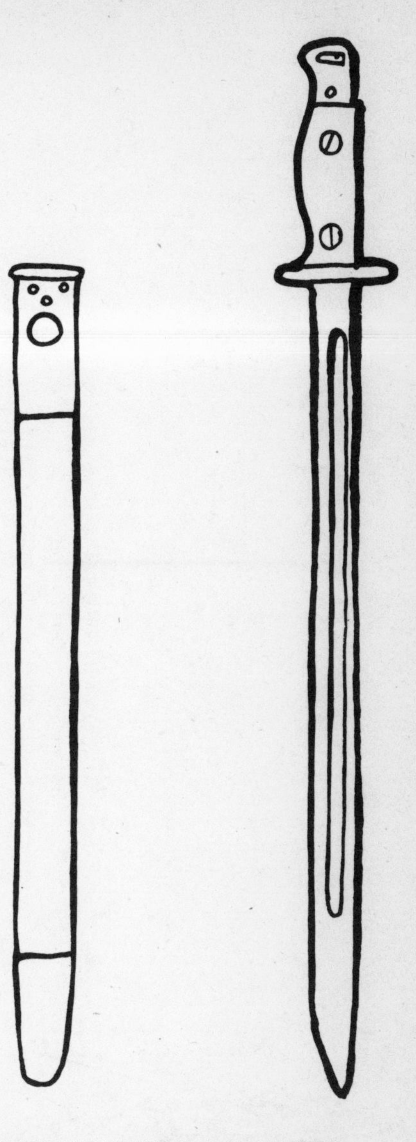

BRITISH PATTERN 1907 SWORD BAYONET AND SCABBARD
The bayonet is the weapon for attack for hand-to-hand fighting. It was often used on night patrols, on sentry duty and for controlling unarmed people, whether they were prisoners or civilians in occupied countries. Probably the most widely used bayonet in history was the British Pattern 1907 sword bayonet.

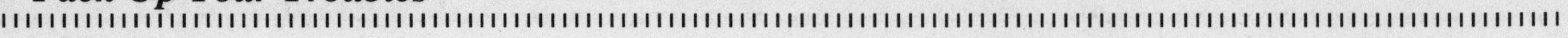

AFTER YOU M'DEAH

Things were getting "just a leedel bit sticky" around "Able" company headquarters of the CBH's one day after the Wehrmacht had made three successive counterattacks. The house the Canadians were in was really taking it. A tank outside had been knocked out by a bazooka, and the next one blew the backdoor down. One more round through the door would be one too many and Corporal A.W. Meacham, Woodstock, Ont., decided something had to be done—but quick. A little rapid calculation and he had it. He opened the front door and the next three bazookas came in one door and out the other, exploding outside. The Jerries went home and "A" Company went on with the war.

The Maple Leaf, Italy Edition, 1944–1945

If Germany and Russia go to war on the Danube that popular waltz, "The Blue Danube," will probably have its title changed to "The Red Danube."

Wings Abroad, 1941

INFANTRY TANK, MK. III, VALENTINE
Valentines were built in Canada from 1941 to1943 by the Canadian Pacific Railway in Montreal. Over 1,400 vehicles were produced. Of these only 30 were retained for training and the rest were delivered to Russia as lend-lease equipment. Three marks of the Valentine tank were built in Canada: Valentine VI, Valentine VII and Valentine VIIA. Considerable development work and redesign was done in Canada on the above three marks of the Valentine.

BACK WITH VENGEANCE

"When I was a little child," the sergeant sweetly addressed his men at the end of an exhaustive hour of drill, "I had a set of wooden soldiers. There was a poor boy in the neighbourhood, and after I had been to Sunday School one day, listening to a stirring talk on the duties of charity, I was soft enough to give them to him. Then I wanted them back and cried, but my mother said: 'Don't cry, Bertie, some day you will get your wooden soldiers back.'

"An believe me, you lop-sided, mutton-headed, goofus-brained set of certified rolling-pins, that day has come!"

Wings Abroad, 1941

We are indebted to Sergeant J.A. Smith, of 405 Squadron, for "letting us in on" a new secret weapon he recently came across. Those who know "Smitty" will appreciate this one… 'Spits' with cans of green paint, which they drop on surfacing U-boat… paint covers periscope lens green.
…Commander, thinking he is still under water, keeps rising…On reaching 2,000 feet 'Spit' shoots him down.

Wings Abroad, 1941

The NAAFI girl was a flirt, and as soon as Corporal Bullman went out to buy a paper she leaned invitingly over the counter with her face close to Rumsam's.

"Now's your chance, darling," she whispered. Rumsam looked around the room. It was empty. So it is, he remarked—and promptly drank the corporal's glass.

Wings Abroad, 1941.

Front-Line Charlie says: "Was 'way up today. Sewed on my GS badge."

The Maple Leaf, Italy Edition, 1944–1945

SURPRISE

The young soldier rushed into the hospital and up to the nurse.

"Quick!" he shouted, "Tell me! Is it a boy?"

"Well," replied the nurse, "the one in the middle is."

Khaki, 1944–1945

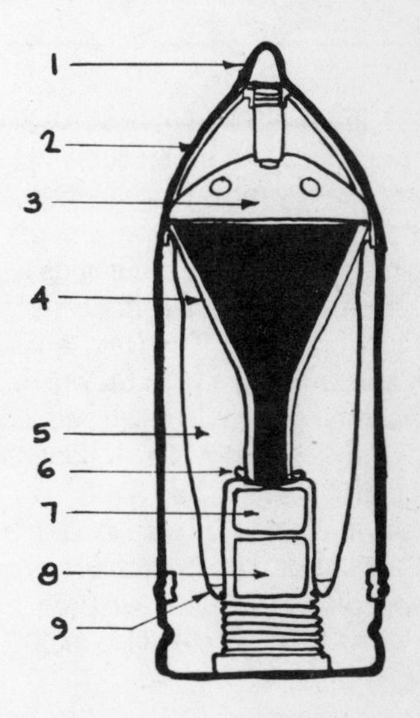

HOLLOW-CHARGE ANTI-TANK SHELL
The Monroe Effect or the Hollow Charge Principle consists of forming a thin-walled shell filled with a high explosive into a cone, then fitting the shell with a suitably shaped nose. Upon detonating the explosive at the rear end focuses the explosive energy of hot gas and finely-divided metal into a "jet" which strikes the target plate. Main parts of a H.E.A.T. round are shown above.

1. Fuze
2. Nose cap
3. Diaphram
4. Steel liner (conical)
5. Charge
6. Copper cup
7. Exploder pellet
8. Tracer
9. Composition

NERVE

One night at the theatre in London, a soldier who had eaten not wisely but too well stood up in his seat right in the middle of the play and called:

"Is there a doctor in the house?"

The actors hesitated a moment then went bravely on.

A few moments later the same Joe still standing, repeated his question.

At this second call another man rose.

"Yes," he said, "I'm a doctor.

Whereupon the soldier enquired thoughtfully: "How do you like the show, Doc?"

Khaki, 1944–1945

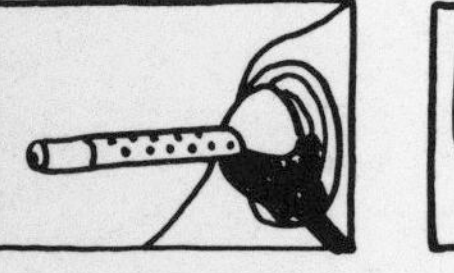

MACHINE GUNS IN TANKS
To provide local AA protection and to engage infantry most tanks carried a secondary armament in the form of machine guns. Typical mountings were in the front, in the mantlet or on the turret roof or cupola. The Ram tank Mk.I and Mk.II carried the U.S. Browning .30 cal. machine gun M1919A. It had a rate of fire of 450-600 rpm. The Valentines produced in Canada had the Besa 7.92 cal. tank machine gun with a rate of fire of 750-850 rpm. The Sexton SP gun had as secondary armament two Bren .303 cal. MG(AA) with a rate of fire of 500 rpm.

EVOLUTION

The soldier who reported on the North African Campaign apparently wasn't kidding when he wrote:

"When you've been here a few weeks, you find yourself talking to yourself. After that you find yourself talking to the lizards. After another couple of weeks you find yourself listening."

Khaki, 1944 –1945

Ali Baba means being away when the crime is committed.

The Beaver Quill, 1942

SWORDFISH

A Canadian divisional headquarters truck with the week's EFI supplies pulled up to a gate late at night. The sentry's challenge rang out:

"Halt! Who goes there?"

"Friend."

"Advance and be recognized."

The truck driver got out and approached the sentry who challenged:

"Beer!"

"No. Sorry lad—none this week," replied the driver.

The Maple Leaf, Italy Edition, 1944

PICKED UP IN PASSING

I never knew they still made 'em this dumb. Was at a headquarters party recently and naturally, in the course of conversation, the Air Force was discussed—and one pretty little gal was labouring under the opinion that every time we took a flip—that WE PAID the pilot seventy-five cents!!!

Wings Abroad, 1941

Small boy, hollering to his mother: "Hey, Mom—you know the vase that you said was passed down from one generation to another?"

"Yes,"

"Well—this generation dropped it!"

Wings Abroad, 1941

285 "SECRET" FLAVOURS.
A popular soft drink back home is reputed to contain 285 secret ingredients, the compounding of which is known only to four men. Well, our local NAAFI dispenses a brownish liquid with only four ingredients and it has 285 different flavours and nobody seems to know how it is made.

Wings Abroad, 1941

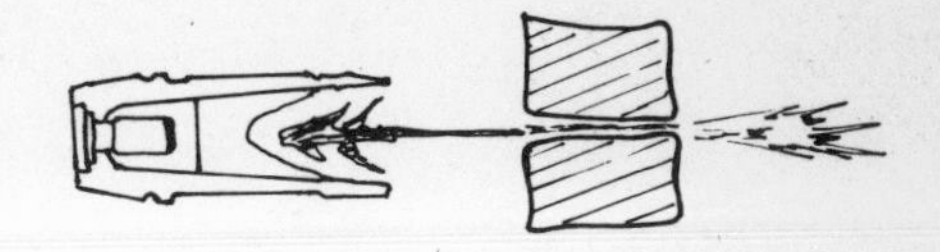

THE HOLLOW CHARGE
When the "jet" of a hollow-charge anti-tank shell strikes the target plate of enemy armour the stream of high-velocity molten debris is under such a great pressure that it blasts a hole through the armor blowing white-hot gases into the tank setting fire to fuel and ammunition and killing or injuring the crew.

Think only of yourself and others will soon forget you.

The Tank, 1943

A man is an animal split half way up and walks on the split end.

The Beaver Quill, 1942

There is no truth in the rumour that whilst on weekend pass, Corporal Jock Howie of the pipe band, found a box of corn plasters, and on coming back to camp tried to get a pair of tight-fitting shoes from stores.

The Tank, 1940

"Now you men," roared the SM, as he dismissed the company, "You will parade again at 2 o'clock precisely. And when I says 2 o'clock precisely, I don't mean five past, I means fives to."

The Beaver Quill, 1942

POEM
The spring is sprung
The grass is riz,
I wonder where the boidies is?
Some say the boids is on the wing.
Now ain't that absoid?
I always hoid
The wings wuz on the boid.

Wings Abroad, 1941

Johnny Nisbet was travelling to Glasgow, and on the way he felt thirsty, so he took out his bottle and drew the cork. Just as he was about to take a taste, a fellow passenger addressed him: "Excuse me, sir, but I am sixty-five years of age and have never tasted a drop of whiskey!"

"Dinna worry yersel'," replied Johnny. "Yer no' gaun to start noo."

Wings Abroad, 1941

A dilapidated airman, his clothing in rags, a shoe missing, his head bandaged and his arm in a sling, was heard to mutter to himself as he shambled away, "I love my country, I'd die for my country. But if ever this damn war is over I'll never love another country!"

Wings Abroad, 1941

SKINK AA TANK
The Skink AA Tank was a variant of the Grizzly I, which in turn was the Canadian-built version of the U.S. M4A1 medium tank. In 1944 the DND contracted with the Waterloo Manufacturing Co. to develop an AA tank on the basis of the Grizzly. The Skink had a modified turret which mounted four 20-mm Polsten cannons and these could be fired simply in salvos of two or all together. Only a few Skinks were completed as the requirement for AA tanks lapsed due to proven Allied air superiority in Europe.

PRESSURE OF WAR ADDS IMPETUS TO INVENTIVE GENIUS.
Vince Meredith creates new laundry method. Washes his laundry in bath tub with rubber boots on. Formulæ:—
1. Pour four inches hot soapy water into tub.
2. Drop in dirty clothes.
3. Put on rubber boots.
4. Get into water
5. Stamp clothes thoroughly.

Result:—"Better than any housewife," says Vince.

Wings Abroad, 1941

HORACE McNUIR'S TESTIMONIAL
"Gentlemen: I was bedridden for six months, a complete physical wreck. Now, since taking three bottles of your Wonderful Medical Discovery, I can climb in and out of the patrol wagon without any assistance whatever."

The Beaver Quill, 1942

"Private Moron saluted a refrigerator, because it was a General Electric."

Khaki, 1943–1944

Strategy is when you don't let the enemy know you are out of ammunition but keep on firing.

WAR PRIZE

"Just because a guy can't round up some eggs is no reason why he should come back empty-handed," is the by-word of Tpr. T.F. Fortey, Douglas, Man. The other day Fortey's squadron leader sent him out on the scrounge for some eggs for the men's and officers' table—especially the officers. His search took him to within a couple of hundred yards of the German lines, but no eggs. Not to be deterred, Fortey ransacked an enemy dump and came up with 600 pounds of Tedeschi sugar—for barter purposes no doubt.

The Maple Leaf, Italy Edition, 1944

CRUISER TANK, RAM MK. I
The Ram Mk. I was the first Canadian devised and built tank. It incorporated the best U.S., British and Canadian ideas of its time. It was manufactured by Montreal Locomotive Works Tank Arsenal from 1941 to1943. The first fifty vehicles housed a British 2-pounder gun and were designated Ram Mk. I. The production vehicles incorporating the 6-pounder and other improvements and modifications were designated Ram Mk. II. Rams were not used in action as gun tanks but were used for training only in Canada or Britain. In 1944 the hulls were to be used as armoured personnel carriers called Kangaroos. Maximum speed was 25 mph and the road radius about 145 miles.

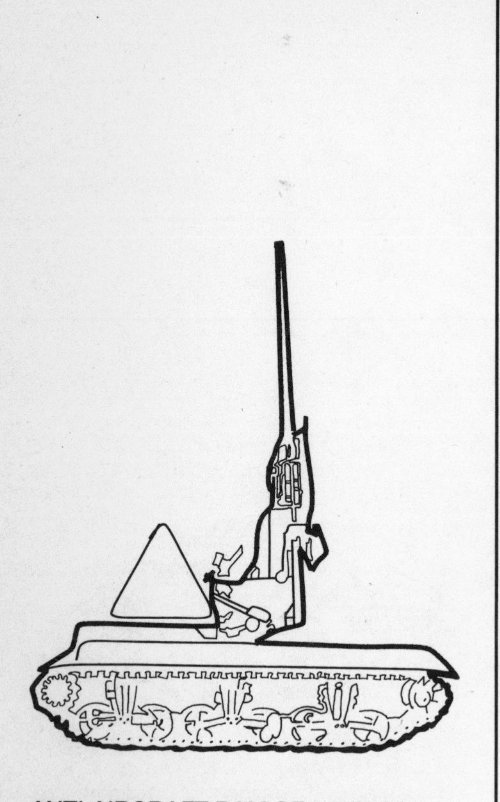

ANTI-AIRCRAFT RAM QF 3.7-IN AA
Only prototypes of this SP equipment were produced. It was an attempt to manufacture a self-propelled mount for the 3.7-inch AA gun using the Canadian Ram tank chassis. The design was not successful even after various modifications and the project was abandoned.

SURPRISE! SURPRISE!
A lieutenant of the West Nova Scotia Regiment forwards a portion of an airletter received from his wife, concerning his five-year-old son, Arthur. The clipping reads: "I must tell you something funny. Arthur was talking to me one day and said he would like to have a little baby brother. I said that we would wait until Daddy came home but he said, "Oh no, let's get one now and surprise Daddy!" "That would be a surprise!"

Comments the officer, "I got quite a laugh out of it."

The Maple Leaf, Italy Edition, 1944

BOOBY-TRAP
The gent with the red face is a signalman with the Eighth Field Regiment. Feeling none too happy about laying a line through an unswept section that might produce a mine or two, if he stepped in the wrong place, the signalman elected to inquire of an Itie standing nearby if he had seen any Germans burying anything lately. The Italian was very obliging and nodded in the affirmative, pointing to an innocent looking piece of ground. The signaller approached gingerly and explored likewise with hesitant fingers in the soil. The Jerry had been burying something. Beneath that innocent soil, a German—latrine.

The Maple Leaf, Italy Edition, 1944

Mary Moron ate some gunpowder for dinner, and then went out and had her hair cut in a bang.

Khaki, 1943–1944

They say there's a new goat in the squadron, but what's new about that? Just because it walks on four legs?

Wings Abroad, 1941

Question—
What did the ceiling say to the walls?
Answer—
Hold me up I'm plastered.

Wings Abroad, 1941

Egbert the AC3: "What's the Scotch Rugby cheer?"
Other Airman: "I dunno, what is it?"
Egbert the AC3: "Get that quarterback."

Wings Abroad, 1941.

Question—
What did one wall say to the other wall?
Answer—
Meet me at the corner and we'll get plastered.

Wings Abroad, 1941

THAT WILL BE THE DAY WHEN —
—The paymaster gives the boys an advance.
—Flight Sergeant McKee gets stuck for words.
—Sergeant Hadden forgets to inspect our barrack rooms.
—The Float Iron Laundry stretches our socks.
—An inspecting officer arrives on time.
—England is without rain for a solid week.
—The 110 stops drinking beer.
—The War is over.

Wings Abroad, 1941

THE FORMULA FOR SUCCESS
Stand up to be seen.
Speak up to be heard.
Shut up to be appreciated.

Wings Abroad, 1941

HOW TO PLAY BRIDGE
Greater Germany's leaders were playing Contract Bridge in Hitler's mountain retreat at Berchtesgaden.

"Three diamonds," said Goering.
"Four spades," said Goebbels.
"Five diamonds," said Von Ribbentrop.
"One club," said Schicklegruber.
"Pass."
"Pass."
"Pass."

Khaki, 1943–1944

ON GUARD
A soldier on his first guard duty halts the officer of the day for routine recognition.

"What would you have done if I hadn't halted?" the officer asked.

"Why, I'd have called the corporal of the guard, sir."

"The corporal of the guard? What for?"

"Well, I'd have called him to help haul your dead carcass away."

Khaki, 1943-1944

THE MESS
The orderly officer entered the men's mess and asked if there were any complaints. A private jumped to his feet.

"Sir, I have a complaint to make. Just taste this."

The officer did and said, "What"s the matter with that? I think that is fine soup."

"Yes, sir, that's what I told the mess sergeant. He said it was coffee."

Khaki, 1943–1944

FINANCE DEPARTMENT
It was a half hour after "lights out" and the night before pay-day. The pay sergeant and his staff were working industriously. From the floor above came the unmistakable sounds of a crap game in progress.

The sergeant turned irritably to one of the privates helping him and said, "Sam, go upstairs and break that crap game."

Sam was gone an hour. He came in with a happy smile.

"Where in blazes were you?" roared the sergeant. "Didn't I tell you to break up that crap game?"

"I did, sarge," Sam replied, "but hell, I only had a quarter to start with."

Khaki, 1943–1944

Front-Line Charlie says: "Was way up yesterday. Went to apply for home leave."

The Maple Leaf, Italy Edition, 1944

"SERVICE WITH A SMILE"
Commanding Officer (on casual inspection to "B" Flight Dispersal Area): "Well, what are you doing here?"
Aircraftsman: "Nothing, Sir," springing to attention from tarpaulin in one leap.
CO: "You may as well be home for all the good you are doing."
AC (breathlessly): "Oh, thank you Sir!"

Wings Abroad, 1940

PROBLEM
Corporal Jenkins and Corporal Moore had received their forty-eight hour passes and were making arrangements. "I'll tell you what," said Jenkins, "let's get our wives together and have a big time."

"Good idea," replied Moore, then hesitated, "but where will we leave them?"

Khaki, 1944–1945

WELL...
Private Jones walked into the canteen just in time to meet his friend George leaving. Jones looked him over and bawled: "Hey, where you going with my raincoat?"
George looked hurt,"You wouldn't want me to get your blouse wet, would you?"

Khaki, 1944–1945

DID YOU KNOW THAT
If every .303 bullet made in Canada in the last year were destined to end the life of a human being, the entire civilised population of the world would be wiped out.

Wings Abroad, 1941

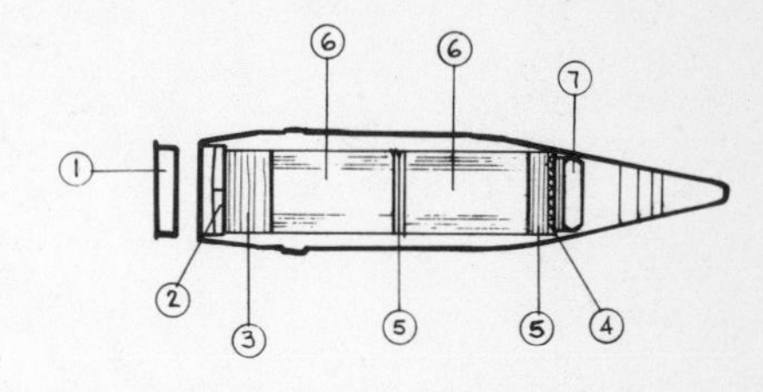

105-MM PROPAGANDA SHELL
1. Rear plug
2. Sealing disc
3. Washers
4. Baffle plate
5. Cardboard discs
6. Rolls of leaflets
7. Bag of black powder

The technique of firing propaganda leaflets in artillery shells over the heads of front line troops was used in World War I and "rediscovered" in North Africa by a British army officer. The leaflets could convey a volume of information and were excellently suited to pictorial presentation. Surrender leaflets and safe conduct passes advised Axis troops that the "shortest route home was through captivity." The method was effectively used in campaigns in Tunisia and Sicily.

WISECRACK OF THE MONTH
"Some of our civil servants aren't civil."

The Beaver Quill, 1942

CAUTION
The officer had been watching the section at pistol practice, and one individual in particular attracted his attention. Calling the Ack I over, he said, "Sergeant, perhaps we had better check the record of that man over there. I notice after every shot he carefully wipes off his fingerprints."

Khaki, 1944–1945

OLD JOKE CORNER
Department Store Santa Claus: "Well, well, well! and what does this little boy want for Christmas?"
Tough little mug: "What the hell's the matter with you, didn't you get my letter?"

The Beaver Quill, 1942

Normally, Homer, I am such a person as does not interfere in the business of others. But I am very curious one day some time ago when I come upon a gathering on a cow path which runs up the Coriano Ridge. Two soldiers and a padre are in a huddle around a hole the boys dig for a dead donk close by.

"It is a funeral for the donk?"

No, Homer, they are having a debate. "And the point in question?"

They are not sure what it is they bury. I hear one guy say it is a mule and the other says no it is a donkey. The padre consults his Bible and says it mentions here it is not a mule and it is not a donkey. It is an ass. "That settles it!" Yes. And the boys go back to dig some more when a CWAC from the Army Show happens along who speaks as follows: Good-day, boys what is that you dig here? A fox-hole?

They say it isn't—according to the Bible.

The Maple Leaf, Italy Edition, 1944

GRAIN OF CORN
Heard about the gal who went to a man's apartment one night? He offered her one of a dozen mink coats.

"What do I have to do?" she asked.

"Just shorten the sleeves."

The Maple Leaf, Italy Edition, 1944

Famous Last Words: "O kay fellows, you can come out now."

FROM THE HOMEFRONT
Owner of a small coffee shop, not doing so well these days, hung this sign on the door: "No coffee, no sugar, no help, no oil, no heat, no profit. If you want a square meal, join the army."

The Maple Leaf, Italy Edition, 1944

En-route to a casualty clearing station for a consultation, one of the wounded men was heard to say, "Gee, I hope it isn't anything trivial."

FLAK—6th Canadian LAA Regiment, 1943–1945

Knowing what to omit, in order to accentuate the rest, is the secret of forceful writing—also of swim suit design.

Wings Abroad, 1940

Customer: "Do you serve women at this bar?"
Bartender: "Nope, you gotta bring your own."

Pilot to air gunner after spraying troops: “Say Smitty, were those guys ever sore when we dived back over them the last time!”
Gunner (dryly): “Small wonder, Sir, you released both containers and left your tail wheel in a lorry cab!”

Wings Abroad, 1940

ADVICE TO THE LOVELORN DEPT.—
Dear Editor:—For the past few months I’ve been asking my girl to marry me and she says “No!” What shall I do?”—Sgnd. Distracted.
Dear Distracted:—“Don’t ask her until Thanksgiving and if she says “No” again…you’ll have something to be thankful for.—Ed.

Wings Abroad, 1940

The absence of black eyes around the airmen’s mess is quite noticeable. “What’s the matter, Doyle, have all the doors been removed?”

Wings Abroad, 1940

If a tank soldier talks of destroying hornets, ants or maggots with his guns, he isn’t wasting ammunition on the insect world. Hornets, ants and maggots are official tank slang for the weapons of the blitzkreig.

Hornets are enemy tanks; ants refer to anti-tank guns; and maggots are machine guns. The terms are used in giving fire orders to tank gunners.

Wings Abroad, 1940

DUAL PERSONALITY
Some army terms are certainly fun
For instance, the “two“ i/c is one!

Khaki, 1943–1944

An ARP Warden was returning from duty when he saw a man doubled up on the white line in the middle of the road. He went over and helped the man to his feet then asked if he was hurt. “Hurt! No,” replied the reveller. “I’m only trying to wind up this bandage.”

The Beaver Quill, October 1941–May 1943

THE KITBAG

THE SOLDIER'S UNABASHED DICTIONARY

Adam's ale—water
Apple polishers—yes-men: those who soft-soap superiors
Act.I—acting instructor or assistant instructor
Agony column—sick parade.
Ack-Acks—anti-aircraft gunners or guns
Angel—the girl friend…
Bath-tub—side-car
Bully—corned beef (also "Bully-beef")
Blood—catsup or chili-sauce
Brew-up—tea (in action, a tank battle)
Bump—a short sharp engagement or fight with the enemy
Browned off—fed up
Brain buster—the Army Examiner
Break-off—to stop work, leave
Chairborne trooper—an administrative soldier
Comedian—a sarcastic NCO
Crawl—sight-seeing with plenty of stops for refreshment
Choir loft—gas chamber (from the instructor's practice of making recruits sing)
Chow—eats
Drill master—a dental officer
Ears—aircraft detectors
Foo—forward observation post officer
F.O. at the H.P.—to leave quickly
Finito—finished (dead)
Gold fish—tinned salmon
Guppie—a CWAC recruit (also new officer in western Canada)
Grenades—meat balls
Going back to Canada—going home on leave
Get cracking—to start moving or working
Grocery boys—supply column
Gestapo—Provost Corps
Holy Joe—a soldier with strong opinions of right and wrong
IDs—identification discs
Joe—a private
Jerk—Anyone at all
Kiltie—a Scots soldier
Lettuce—paper money
Lettuce line—pay parade
Lead swinger—a soldier who fakes hard work or loafs on duty
Moe—the Medical Officer (from initials "M" and "O")

"The Canadians are Best"

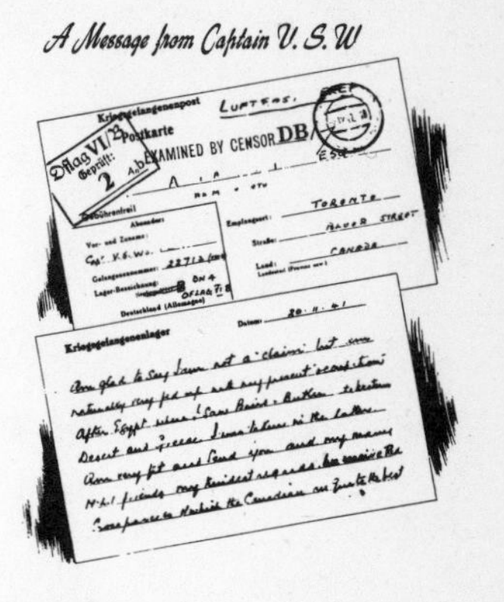

Reproduced above is a "Prisoner of War" card received from Captain V.S.W., who had been a POW in Germany since the campaign in Greece in 1942. The captain says: "We receive Red Cross parcels of which the Canadian are quite the best."

Mud—coffee
Muzzle—gas respirator
Mick—Irish soldier
Meatball—a fat guy
Nuts—Nuts!
One-pip wonder—a 2nd lieutenant
Old Man—the commander of a company
On the peg—up for discipline
Pearl diver—dish washer
P.B.I.—infantry
Pill roller—medical orderly
Quiz kid—an over-anxious recruit
Retread—a veteran serving for the second time
Romper—fatigue coveralls
Reading Room—the latrine
Snake charmer—bagpiper
Side arms—knife and fork
Shyster—a guy who thinks he knows all the angles in Army life
Scalper— army barber

Sally Ann—Salvation Army lassie
Shower curtain—gas cape
Tinned cow—condensed milk
Tick off—to reprimand
Taffy—a Welshman
Tommy—an Englishman
Ubangi—a loud talker or gossip
Worms—spaghetti
Zombie—non-Active soldier

The sentry challenged a uniformed figure entering the camp.

"Colonel Rogers," came the reply.

"Sorry, sir," said the sentry, "I can't let you proceed without the password."

The other snorted. "Good heavens, man, I've forgotten it, but you know me well enough".

The sentry persisted, doing his duty. "Can't help it sir, I must have the password".

"Don't stand there arguin' all night, Bill!" came a voice from the guardhouse. "Shoot him!"

Khaki, 1943–1944

Private Pashkoodnik had just passed his plate up for a sixth helping of roast beef, gravy and potatoes.

The man on his left was impressed. "Brother," he murmured, "you sure like your food".

"Not at all," replied Private Pashkoodnik modestly. "I just happen to be passionately devoted to bicarbonate of soda".

Khaki, 1943–1944

A brigadier, a colonel and a major were having a heated argument one night on the subject of matrimony. The brigadier maintained that marriage was 60% work and 40% fun. The colonel said it was 75% work and 25% fun. The major insisted that it was 90% work and 10% fun. At the height of the argument an orderly appeared at the door. "Let's leave it to him," said the major. The orderly listened carefully to the argument and said with an air of absolute finality:

"If you will pardon me, sirs, matrimony is 100% fun and no work at all."

"How do you figure that?" asked the astonished officers.

"It's very simple," replied the orderly. "If there was any work in it at all, you guys would have me doing it."

Khaki, 1943–1944

In a recent medical checkup Jack "Downbeat" Robertson was stark naked before the MO when Staff Sergeant Clark quipped, "What's that, another German atrocity?"

FLAK—6th Canadian LAA Regiment, 1943–1945

DID YOU KNOW THAT
A good sniper can knock off a cigarette smoker at 300 yards in the dark.

Wings Abroad, 1941

ENVY
Oh, I wish I were a deciduous tree
Because it gets more leaves than me.

Khaki, 1943–1944

MOTOR TORPEDO BOAT—MTB
In 1944 the RCN formed two flotillas of MTBs which were equipped with the 72-foot "G" type and the 115-foot "D" type of boat. The "G" type had a maximum speed of 41 knots and the "D" type had a maximum speed of 30 knots. The small, fast and highly manoeuvrable MTBs took part in a variety of operations in the English Channel and off the coast of France, carrying out night attacks on enemy coastal shipping, blockading enemy harbours and guarding the flanks of the invasion beaches. Armament consisted of 6 pounder pom-pom gun, small automatics, torpedoes and/or depth charges.

What treasurer of what Royal Canadian Air Force newspaper recently made a business trip to Glasgy Toon and there was approached by a poor, tattered, old heather seller, and when he found the price was tuppence, took pity and paid sixpence only to hear the peddler to go further down the alley hollering "Heather-r-r-r, a penny each!"? Listen, Calgary Cowboy. When are you going to learn that the "Canada" on your shoulder automatically doubles the price and you're not required to tip?

Wings Abroad, 1941

A smart man is one who hasn't let a woman pin anything on him since he was a baby.

Wings Abroad, May 1941

We have heard that serious thought has been given to the exchanging of two wireless men for a trained parrot that will say, "Hello Bonzo, this is Bozo calling—over."

Wings Abroad, 1941

SECRET AMBITION
To be able to learn and understand the lingo of:—
(A) The newspaper seller.
(B) The platform attendant calling off the names of stations.
(C) A cockney drinking beer.

Wings Abroad, 1941

Something in common with a few million people in this country—I got a bomb story…

Wings Abroad, 1941

Mayotte: "What did the ocean say to the shore?"
Swain: "I'll bite. What?"
Mayotte: "Not a thing, just waved."

Wings Abroad, 1941

"Oh, why can't it wait and go off with the bugle?"

It has been said with some truth that when a soldier stops grumbling about everything in general, there is something seriously wrong with his morale. If this is a reliable yardstick, the writer has seen little evidence of a decline in that of the average Canadian Soldier.

FLAK—6th Canadian LAA Regiment, 1943–1945

The editor certainly won't let this one get by; it was turned down by the editor of a well-known imperial regiment's magazine and will doubtless suffer the same fate now. You all know the old saying "Up with the lark?" Well, I gather that the modern equivalent of that, in the England of today, is "To bed with the wren."

The Beaver Quill, 1942

The Department of Agriculture is seeking to find out the extent to which goats are kept in Canada. Janitors of lodge rooms will please report at once.

The Beaver Quill, 1942

One of Germany's best sellers is that American masterpiece, "How to Make Friends and Influence People."

Wings Abroad, 1941

REMEMBER
Military Clerks.
Hear and see a lot.
They know a lot, but say not what.
ZIPS ON LIPS, SAVE MEN AND SHIPS.

The Beaver Quill, 1942

OFF THE RECORD
RCE officer: "There's an unexploded bomb buried here probably weighing more than a ton. Just keep an eye on it and blow your whistle if anything happens."
"OK?" replied the private, "but do I blow it going up or coming down?"

The "Big 2" Bugle (QOR of C), 1944

MORALE
Good morale is doing without something one wants very badly.

The Beaver Quill, 1942

DID YOU KNOW?
The name of the dainty airman who asked the Army laundry to have his pyjamas washed in Lux? (Do you Lux your undies?)

Wings Abroad, 1940

Famous Last Words: "Let's kick it and see?"

A timid soul was speaking to a paratrooper.
"You must be awfully brave. I can't understand how you are able to hang from that silk thing. Isn't the suspense terrible?"
"Nope, lady," came the nonchalant reply. "It's when the suspense ain't there that it's terrible.

Khaki, 1943–1944

Then there's the letter a Canadian stationed "Somewhere—where—it's—very chilly" wrote to his parents: "It's so cold here that the inhabitants have to live somewhere else."

Khaki, 1943–1944

Another soldier tried to show the difference between a lieutenant and a drill sergeant to his parents. "It's easily explained. My lieutenant has pips on his shoulder; my sergeant has a chip."

Khaki, 1943–1944

Two soldiers had been off on a glorious all-night toot. When one of them regained consciousness, the sun was shining brightly and he was lying in a hospital completely swathed in bandages. His bleary-eyed friend was sitting by the bed-side, regarding him dolefully.
"What happened to me, Tom?" mumbled the stricken one.
"Well," replied his friend, "we were sitting peacefully in a room on the 6th floor of the Avalon Hotel when suddenly you jumped to the ledge of the window and roared: 'Here's where I fly down Main Street!'"
"What! Why didn't you stop me?" asked the bandage indignantly.
"Stop you?" was the reply. "What do you mean stop you? I thought you could do it."

Khaki, 1943–1944

Advice to senior NCOs: "Why bark when you've got a dog around?"

Wings Abroad, 1941

On the church steps after a wedding ceremony.
—Who gave the bride away?
—I could have but I kept my mouth shut.

The Beaver Quill, 1941–1942

My throat is dry, my tongue is parchin'
Parades are better to watch than marchin'

There was the sailor who treated all his girls with wine. He wanted a little port in every sweetheart.

The study of the sex life of a snail would, I am sure, reveal most interesting characteristics. Whatever there is about a pair of leather boots left unworn for a day that breaks down the maidenly modesty of the female snail, Heaven only knows! The shocking scenes that have taken place on my spare pair of boots defy description.

FLAK—6th Canadian LAA Regiment, 1943–1945

He: "Why is it you have so many boy friends?"
She: "I give up."

The Beaver Quill, 1941–1943

Q: "What is the best thing to have when the bombs fall?"
A: "Presence of mind? No. Absence of body."

The Beaver Quill, 1941–1943

False doctrine means giving people the wrong medicine.

The Beaver Quill, 1942

A circle is a round line with no kinks in it and joined up so as not to show where it began.

The Beaver Quill, 1942

"Halt!! Who goes there?"
"Air Force Chaplain."
"Advance, Charlie Chaplin, to be recognised and don't be so _____ funny next time."

Wings Abroad, 1941

COMMON GROUND
A voluntary effort by men of the British Columbia Dragoons in cleaning up a bombed out private chapel resulted recently in what the unit's padre Hon. Captain H.A. Marklinger, Vancouver, termed "one of the most satisfying and successful services I have ever conducted." Desirous of a church service on the Sunday following the capture of Castiglione di Cervia the men went to work after their padre received permission to use the chapel from the local parish priest. Unable to speak Italian H-Capt. Marlinger used Latin as the conversational medium. "I understood the priest very well," he said, "but my own Latin grammar was rather rusty. However he understood me all right." The service, which was voluntary, was attended by an overflow crowd. The chapel, later that morning, was used by the priest for a service attended by the town's inhabitants.

The Maple Leaf, Italy Edition, 1944–1945

A soldier displaying considerable worry about his first trip "over the top" was questioned by his captain regarding his fear.

The man revealed that he was desperately afraid his belly button would be shot away.

"Why worry over your belly button?" asked the officer.

"Well," replied the private, "I've a bad habit of eating celery in bed and if my belly button is shot away where am I going to put the salt?"

Wings Abroad, 1941

FICTIONARY (unabashed)
Ex-pectre-ate: To drool at a ghoul.
Disasster: Falling off a donkey.

The "Big 2" Bugle, 1944

GOEBBEL'S GOBBLE
Just after the *Scharnhorst* was sunk, Moscow's "Red Star" published a cartoon showing a forlorn sailor disappearing into the sea. In the foreground Propaganda Minister Goebbels shouts into a microphone: "We won a great victory. The German underseas fleet has increased in one stroke by 26,000 tons."

Khaki, 1944–1945

DID YOU KNOW THAT
The glow of a lighted match can be clearly seen at 900 yards.

Wings Abroad, 1941

It is estimated that the average number of bacteria on a dollar bill is 142,000.

Wings Abroad, 1941

SIMPLE DEFENCE WORKS
Concealment from air and ground observation, as well as a good view of the ground or target to be covered by fire, is of importance when choosing defensive positions. Some of the more common terms used in describing a fire trench are shown:

1. Parador
2. Berm
3. Rear slope
4. Fire step
5. Interior slope
6. Elbow rest
7. Crest
8. Parapet
9. Superior slope
10. Exterior slope

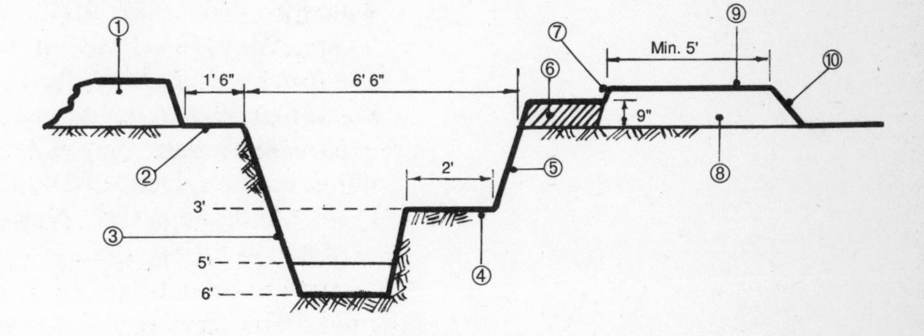

Sources

Air Burst, Jun., Jul. 1945.
The Beaten Zone , Aug., Sep, Nov. 1945.
The Beaver Quill, Oct., Nov., Dec. 1941, Mar., Apr., May, Jun., Jul., Aug., Oct., Nov. 1942, Feb., May 1943.
The Beret, Jan. 1946.
The "Big 2" Bugle, Jul., Aug., Sep., Oct. 1944 (Nos. 11-62).
The Bullet, Jan., Feb., Mar., Apr., May 1944.
Canada at War, Jan. 1942, Feb., Mar. 1944.
Canadian Air Cadet, Nov. 1941, Nov. 1942.
The Canadian Red Cross Junior, Apr., May, Nov., Dec. 1942.
The Column Courier, 1 Canadian Army Transport Column, Aug., Oct. 1944, Feb., Apr., Jun., Mar. 1945.
CWAC News Letter, May, Sep., Oct., Dec. 1944, Jan., May, Jun. 1945, Spring 1945.
Despatch, The Official Journal of the Canadian Red Cross Society, Jan., Mar.-Apr., May-Jun., Jul.-Aug. 1940, Jan.-Feb. 1942, Jan.-Feb., Apr.-May, Sep. 1943.
Facts and Figures Weekly, Jun., Jul. Sep. 1944, Mar. 1945.
FLAK, Official Weekly Bulletin of 6th Canadian LAA Regiment – Royal Canadian Artillery, 1943–1944.
Inco Triangle, Jul., Aug., Oct., Dec. 1939.
Khaki—The Army Bulletin, May, Jun., Jul., Sep. 1943, Jan., Feb. 1944.
The Legionary, May 1952, Feb. 1953.
The Mailed Fist, May 1938.
The Maple Leaf, Mar., Nov., Dec. 1944, Jan., Feb., Mar., 1945.
The Maple Leaf—Italy Edition, Jan, Feb., Mar., Apr., May, Jun., Jul., Aug. Sep., Oct., Nov. 1944
The Tank—Canada, Official Journal of the Canadian Armoured Corps, , Nov., Dec. 1940, Mar., Aug., Oct. 1941, Feb., Apr., May, Jun. 1943.
The Ranger, Jan., May, Jun. 1943.
Royal Canadian Navy Monthly Review (R.C.N.M.R.), Aug., Nov. 1942, Jan., Aug., Oct. 1943, Mar. 1944.
Wings Abroad, Dec. 1940, Jan., Feb., Mar., Apr., May, Jun., Jul., Aug., Sep., Oct., Nov., Dec. 1941, Jan., Mar. 1942, Mar. 1943, Sep. 1944.